Dr. Nedley's
Depression

Recovery
Program ™
Workbook

Neil Nedley, M.D.

An eight-part series that reveals the keys to achieving peace of mind and restoring energy, joy and satisfaction to your life.

Nedley Publishing
P.O. Box 1565
Ardmore, OK 73402

(888) 778-4445
(580) 226-8007

ISBN 978-0-966-1979-8-4

Caution: This book and video series does not establish a doctor–patient relationship with the reader. Persons who are ill or on medication who wish to significantly change their lifestyle should do so under the direction of a physician familiar with the effects of lifestyle change on health.

Cover and Interior Design by Brent Bechtel

Special thanks to Paula Marie Reiter and Christopher Kelly—among many others whose time and devotion allowed for the completion of this manual.

Thanks to the Florida Center for Instructional Technology for providing the use of several images included in this workbook.

Contents

Welcome to the Nedley Depression Recovery Program

CONGRATULATIONS on purchasing the most comprehensive program available on the subject of depression recovery. Learn well the lessons set before you, because they are life to you.

Whether you or a loved one are struggling with depression or other mental health challenges, there is good news. Depression should not be tolerated as a lifelong condition—and this is why the Nedley Depression Recovery Program focuses on the underlying and contributing causes of depression—so that a lasting cure can be found. In order to participate, you need to have a willingness to adapt your diet and lifestyle, as well as your mental thought patterns.

If you are viewing this at home, set aside two hours, one day a week—preferably the same day each week—for the next eight weeks in order for this program to be the most beneficial. (For example: Monday 7–9 PM; Tuesday morning, 6–8 AM.)

Also note that this program should be viewed as a mental health series concerned with educating and aiding individuals on the path to recovery. The Nedley Depression Recovery Program is not a substitute for a physician, psychiatrist, or a counselor, and if you are in need of help from such sources, you should not hestitate to seek it.

Nedley Clinic offers a Nedley 10-day Residential Depression Recovery Program. For more information go to www.drnedley.com. There are also 8-week Depression Recovery Programs available in select cities, operated by those trained by Dr. Nedley to administer his program. If you feel that participation in a hands-on experience would be of additional benefit to you, then you should feel free to make arrangements to attend one of these programs.

A Word from Dr. Nedley

Due to the response from my book, *Depression: the Way Out*, and the subsequent success of the Nedley Depression Recovery Program—an eight-week series about overcoming depression through lifestyle change——I receive more requests to speak than one person can handle. I decided that the best way to get this message of health to those who need it most would be to produce a recorded series of my live presentations along with the materials the participants receive. This allows any person, from the comfort of their home, to take advantage of the 20-Week Turn Around that I outline in the book.

This workbook is designed to be used in connection with the DVD series and my book, *Depression: the Way Out*. Two depression Self Tests are included in your workbook. I also recommend you take the Comprehensive Depression, Anxiety, and EQ Assessment, either online or ask the person directing your 8-week program for a copy of the assessment. Make sure to include your full name, address and date of birth. This will provide us with important data which will not only benefit yourself, but others who suffer from this unfortunate and often debilitating disease.

Neil Nedley, M.D.
Ardmore, Oklahoma
January, 2005

About This Book

The Nedley Depression Recovery Program Workbook is an aid to your success in recovering from depression. This workbook has been designed to include all of the primary aspects that are addressed when attending a live presentation of the program given by Dr. Nedley.

These important parts of the program include:

• **Reading Prescriptions**, which are designed to prepare you for the material included in the presentations (as well as to reinforce the ideas contained therein). Reading the prescribed chapters will allow you to have more familiarity with the concepts presented in each session, so you will benefit even more from what Dr. Nedley discusses.

• **Printed versions of the PowerPoint™ slides** that Dr. Nedley uses in his presentations. This will help you follow along more closely and take notes, as well as fill in the missing blanks on the slides in your book. (Don't worry, the answers are in the back of the workbook.)

• **Highlights** and key points of the presentations.

• **Daily Doses** which describe the nutrients, water intake and other components necessary for a full recovery from depression.

• **Lifestyle Matters** bring forth Dr. Nedley's lessons into practical, easy to implement activities which can be incorporated into your own life in a fun, safe and successful manner.

Dr. Nedley's Suggested Reading List

Depression: the Way Out by Neil Nedley, M.D.

The Lost Art of Thinking by Neil Nedley, M.D.

SOS: Help for Emotions—Managing Anxiety, Anger & Depression
by Lynn Clark, Ph.D.

Telling Yourself the Truth: Find Your Way out of Depression, Anxiety, Fear, Anger, and Other Common Problems by Applying the Principles of Misbelief Therapy
by William Backus, Ph.D. and Marie Chapian

Feeling Good: The New Mood Therapy by David D. Burns, M.D.

Mind, Character and Personality, Volumes 1 and 2 by E.G. White

At Jesus' Feet: The Gospel According to Mary Magdalene by Doug Batchelor

The Feeling Good Handbook by David D. Burns, M.D.

The Passion of Love: He Did it for You by E.G. White

Broken Chains: Finding Peace for the Raging Soul by Doug Batchelor

Success demands aim—
success in any line demands a definite aim.
You must keep a steady view of what you are aiming for.

છ૭

As you listen to the presentations and begin doing the assignments, keep in mind the story of the crow found on the next page. Each assignment, no matter how insignificant you think it may be, must be followed to reach success.

Please read the testimony on page 50 to understand the importance of doing everything as directed.

Refer to "Small Ideas for Making a Big Difference in Your Wellness" from time to time as your improvement continues and as you incorporate wellness concepts into your life.

Small Ideas for Making a Big Difference in Your Wellness

esop once told the story of a crow, half-dead from thirst, who came upon a vase with just a little water in the bottom. Try as he might, the crow could not reach the precious water with his short beak. At the moment he was ready to give up in despair, he had an idea. He picked up a pebble and dropped it into the vase. Still he couldn't reach the water. So he dropped another pebble into the vase. Then another. And another. And another. One by one, the crow dropped pebbles into the vase, until the water level rose and he could take a drink and save his life.

Small Things Can Make a Big Difference

Are you like the crow? Do you focus on big problems and lofty goals and forget that little things can make a huge difference in your life? Instead of stretching, straining, and sometimes failing, why not focus on a few small things, like adding pebbles to a vase? Working on a couple of small goals consistently over time can help you bring about even bigger changes.

Take a look at the ideas we've listed on the next four pages. You'll find plenty of small things that can make a big difference in your family, social, and inner wellness. Admittedly, none of these things will do much to change the world. But if you stick to them, you just might change your world.

Five Ways to Improve Your Family Wellness

1. Eat your evening meal together in your own home at least four nights a week. Make sure every member of the immediate family is present. Use the time to talk about what happened that day (at work, at school, on the playground, in your home). Turn off the TV and take your time to relax, eat, and talk.

2. Schedule uninterrupted family time at least one afternoon or evening every week. Use the time to play a game together, plan a vacation, go on a walk, or resolve family issues. Wrestle with your kids, play tag, read a story, write letters, make cookies, or just sit and talk. Don't answer the phone, and leave the TV off. If you block out the same time every week, you'll be more likely to stick with it as the weeks go by.

3. Plant and maintain a family garden. Grow your own vegetables and flowers. Give everyone a chance to plant, weed, and harvest what you grow. Teach your children what's involved in maintaining healthy plants. And make sure everyone gets a taste of the fruits of your labor.

4. Go on occasional "dates" with your children. This is about creating one-on-one relationships with each of your children, not spending a lot of money or buying them presents. Go to the park and swing. Pack a couple of sandwiches and go for a short hike. Or simply give your child the choice of what to do for an hour or two.

5. Hire a sitter occasionally for an adults-only date. Strong families start with healthy adults who take good care of themselves. If you're not living with a spouse, call a friend to join you for a craft show or a game of racquetball. Adults need time away from kids (and time at work doesn't count).

Five Ways to Improve your Intellectual Wellness

1. Turn off the TV. The average American household spends eight hours a day watching TV. And while television can expose you to new ideas and important information, chances are you could put some of that time to better use. Kids need to develop cognitive skills (which they learn from play, not watching TV) and adults can benefit by replacing TV with real social interaction. What's worse, TV may be making you fat. According to the Journal of the American Medical Association, every two hours spent watching TV increases your risk of obesity by 23%.

2. Spend time focusing on the positive. Whether you spend that time meditating, reading, playing music, or simply thinking, this time gives you space to step away from the overwhelming stimuli of the day and recharge and reconnect with your feelings. Let yourself wonder, wander, laugh, be happy and simply see the world as it is.

3. Take a class. As you learn new skills and information, your brain forms new cells and makes new connections between existing neurons. Try a course in self-defense, photography, writing, or history. Check with your local college or university for a list of continuing education classes that are open to the public. And if you don't live near a college, there are hundreds of options for learning online.

4. Develop a talent. Always wanted to play the piano but never took the time? Why not do it now? Or take up painting, woodworking, or cooking. Just as exercise works your muscles, learning new skills works your brain.

5. Look for new ideas. It's easy to get stuck in a rut—doing the same things day after day. Break out by looking for fresh ideas and new perspectives. Visit the magazine rack at your local bookstore, but instead of picking up your favorites, read a few magazines you've never seen before. Better still, browse through a magazine that argues the opposite political view from the one you hold. You don't have to agree—simply explore a different perspective and new ideas.

Four Ways to Improve Your Social Wellness

1. Start a book group. Invite a few people
   to read the same book at the same
   time and get together once a week
   to discuss and reflect. This is a great
   way to stretch your mind and interact with others. You'll probably
   read a few books you'd never have
   found on your own. More importantly, you'll meet and make
   friends with people you wouldn't
   have found otherwise. *(For Dr. Nedley's
   recommended reading list, see page viii.)*

2. Write a letter. Letter writing was once the only way to communicate with far-
   away friends and relatives. Today we've lost that tradition and the opportuni-
   ties to express to our loves ones how we feel about them. Take a few minutes
   to write to an old teacher, friend, or distant family member and let them
   know how they've touched your life. E-mail is a good start, but a handwrit-
   ten letter will have a more lasting effect.

3. Go to a symphony, classical music concert, or church social. To be socially
   well, you need to get out and be around people. Why not gather with a few
   friends for dinner? Or get cheap seats at the symphony. Make sure you leave
   time afterwards to enjoy the company. After all, that's the whole reason to go
   out in the first place.

4. Meet your neighbors. Today's lifestyles make it easy to live life without ever
   getting to know the people who live around us. Take a few minutes to get
   to know them. Stop by with some Maple Walnut cookies (Appendix X of
   Depression: the Way Out), invite them over for an Oat Burger (same section)
   or simply stop by to say hello. You'll enjoy your neighborhood more and you
   just might discover a few friends.

Four Ways to Improve Your Physical Wellness

1. Make time for exercise. I recommend that you get at least 30–60 minutes of exercise a day. In addition to exercising to relieve your depression, simply plan time each day for an activity you enjoy—walk around a park, jump on the trampoline, ride your bike, play tennis or basketball. Exercise doesn't have to be drudgery, just get out and move. You'll decrease your depression, help prevent a laundry list of diseases, and even reverse some aspects of aging with daily exercise. Better still, do it with a friend!

2. Get a regular check-up from a doctor. Find a good doctor and make your health a priority. Many diseases, like diabetes, heart disease, and high blood pressure, can be treated and even prevented if discovered early enough. You should begin a regular schedule of physicals by the time you are 30. Working with your doctor, plan a regular schedule for check-up, screenings, and other tests that just may save your life.

3. Reduce your stress. Take a walk, pray, meditate, or stretch. Researchers say people who build stress-busting habits into their daily routine have a big health advantage over those who don't. Unhealthy stress can put you at risk for all kinds of chronic diseases. Eliminating unnecessary stressful situations from your life can have a big impact on your health.

4. Spend time in nature. You will find that there is much to enjoy walking by a stream, hiking up a mountain, breathing fresh country air, and relaxing on bright, sunny days. Incorporate sunshine, deep breathing, drinking water, and exercising into your daily schedule.

Self-Evaluations

Please complete the **Depression Self Test before proceeding. A more comprehensive assessment that measures presence and severity of depression, brain hit areas, anxiety level, and emotional intelligence (EQ) is available at www.drnedley.com.**

Depression Self Test—"Before"

Reflect over the previous two weeks and rate the following symptoms:
(Circle the appropriate number for each item.)

	A None	B Questionable	C Mild	D Definite
1. Deep sadness or feelings of emptiness; feeling down or hopeless.	0	1	2	3
2. Decreased interest or pleasure in nearly all activities.	0	1	2	3
3. Decrease or increase in appetite; or unusual loss or gain in weight.	0	1	2	3
4. Sleep habits have changed; sleeping more or less than usual.	0	1	2	3
5. Others (or you) have noticed your physical movements or speech have been slower than normal; or instead that you have more agitation or irritation with yourself or others.	0	1	2	3
6. Experiencing fatigue or loss of energy; feeling tired often.	0	1	2	3
7. Experiencing feelings of worthlessness, inappropriate guilt, or that you are a failure.	0	1	2	3
8. Decrease in ability to think or concentrate on common tasks or difficulty making good decisions.	0	1	2	3
9. Thinking about death often or considering harming yourself or others.	0	1	2	3

Self-Scoring the Depression Self Test

Add the numbers from each column above, and place the totals in the corresponding boxes here—then add across to determine your final symptom score for the Self Test.

Examples: Since column A is always equal to 0 (zero), this blank is already filled with a zero. If you circle four "1"s in column B, then your total for that column is "4". If you circle three "2"s in column C, then your total for that column is "6". If you circle nine "3"s in column D, then your total for that column is "27". *(These are all hypothetical totals.)*

A __0__ + B _____ + C _____ + D _____ = _____
                                                                    Total Score

If you answered B, C, or D for Question 9, be sure to see a health professional *as soon as possible,* even if it means going to the local Emergency Room.

Major depression is a concern if you have answered questions 1 or 2 with B, C, or D *and* have a score as indicated below:

0–6 .... None
7–10 .... Mild
11–19 .... Moderate
20 or above .... Severe

Please Note: Having recently faced a dramatic emotional crisis or loss can cause situational depression or bereavement. **This test is not designed to replace the competent evaluation of a health professional.**

Now anyone can measure:

- Emotional Intelligence (EQ)
- Anxiety level
- Presence and severity of depression
- Individual brain "Hit" Areas

With Dr. Nedley's Comprehensive Depression, Anxiety, and EQ Assessment, you can:

- Track your progress anytime
- Watch for warning signs in your spouse or other family members
- Identify the major contributing factors that may be leading to depression
- Determine if your anxiety levels are in the abnormal range
- Test your own E.Q.---then watch the score go up as you seek to improve it!

This one-of-a-kind assessment, developed at the Nedley Clinic, is the result of countless hours of study and clinical experience. Because of the significant investment Nedley Solutions has made in scanning equipment and scoring software, there is a minimal charge for taking the assessment.

Health

It may be taken online anonymously at drnedley.com. It is also available in an "Iowa Skills" type format to be given at seminars or in group settings.
The "Iowa Skills" format test must be returned to Nedley Health Solutions for scoring (turnaround time is usually one week). Online tests receive an immediate score. (Please print your results)

Call today! (888) 778-4445 or visit www.drnedley.com

SIMPLY BETTER. SIMPLY DELICIOUS. SIMPLY HEALTHY.

Omega-3 Uplift Bar

Developed from the scientifically validated nutritional information in Dr. Nedley's books, the Omega-3 Uplift bar is the tasty and convenient way to feed your brain. The uplift bar fights depression by providing a reliable source of Omega-3, calcium, tryptophan, folic acid and vitamin B12.

To maintain optimal brain health you need 3,000 mg of Omega-3 per day. One Maple Walnut Uplift Bar provides 3,000 mg of Omega-3, while the Almond Butternut flavored bar provides 2,500 mg and the Almond Chip provides 1,500 mg.

For Heart Health

Omega-3 can help decrease blood pressure, lower triglycerides, decrease the stickiness of platelets, and reduce the risk of clotting--in turn helping to reduce the risk of a heart attack.

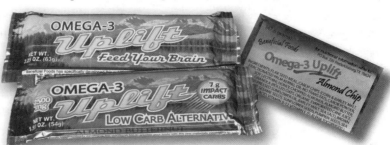

For Depression

Omega-3 fats are emerging as an important nutritional element in brain science. A diet high in omega-3 decreases the risk of depression. Abundant omega-3 is found in flax seeds, walnuts, and almonds--and the Uplift Bar contains all three. Omega-3 Uplift bar is also a goo dsource of calcium, tryptophan, folic acid, and vitamin B_{12}--all kknown to help alleviate symptoms of depression.

For Kids

Omega-3 fatty acids are necessary for optimal brain development and life-long health--of crucial importance to mothers who are pregnant or raising young children. The effects of Omega-3 deficiency last a lifetime as well. Omega-3 is an essential fat in anyone's diet, and omega-3 contained in the Uplift bar is beneficial to both the pregnant or nursing mother and her child.

A Perfect Solution

Developed from the scientifically validated nutritional information in Dr. Nedley's books, *Proof Positive*, and *Depression: the Way Out*, the Omega-3 Uplift bar is the tasty and convenient way to feed your brain. Whether you're concerned about general well-being, cardiovascular health, your children's health, or just need a lift, the Uplift bar provides an easy answer.

Scientific studies have shown Omega-3 fats to:

- Maximize IQ
- Build serotonin levels
- Decrease blood pressure
- Lower triglycerides

- Decrease the risk of depression
- Promote optimal brain development for children
- Aid in disease prevention, and
- Have anti-inflammatory properties.

Call today! (888) 778-4445 or visit www.drnedley.com

Nedley Health Solutions
offers a

10-day Nedley Residential Depression Recovery Program

A Perfect Place to Heal.

You will enjoy 10 days away from the everyday stresses of life in a calm, comfortable environment. In addition to a caring staff, life-changing presentations, and an energizing routine--

The Program Includes

- Lifestyle treatment for depression
- One-on-one consultation with Dr. Nedley
- Comprehensive health history review
- Counseling sessions
- Techniques for behavior change
- Help with overcoming addictions
- Support for dealing with loss
- Delicious healthy meals
- Instruction on food choices and preparation
- Diagnostic laboratory services
- Aerobic conditioning
- Flexibility training
- Daily interactive presentations
- Stress management

For more info call (888) 778-4445 or visit www.drnedley.com

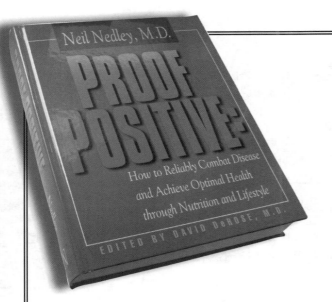

Books by Neil Nedley, M.D.

Dr. Nedley, author of the Depression Recovery Program has also authored the best-selling books Proof Positive and Depression: The Way Out.

Dr. Nedley's latest book is *The Lost Art of Thinking: Improving Emotional Intelligence and Mental Performance.*

New The Lost Art of Thinking

Who wouldn't like to achieve peak mental perfomance? Order this ground-breaking book, and benefit from Dr. Nedley's unique perspective on how to clear up cognitive distortions and maximize your thinking potential--from physical, mental, and spiritual points of view.

This revolutionary new book combines highly effective cognitive behavioral therapy techniques with positive lifestyle choices and reveals the balanced approach which has been so stunningly successful in helping so many achieve peak mental performance. This is a must-read!

Proof Positive

This landmark book tells, in easy to understand language, how to fight disease and achieve optimal health through proper lifestyle and nutrition. It offers outstanding resource material and is packed with eye-catching visual aids. Learn how to reverse heart disease, diabetes and blocked arteries.

Gain understanding about the relationship between melatonin and a good night's sleep, and receive vital information about cancer prevention and boosting your immune system. This fascinating book has had a profound impact on the lives, and health, of many people.

Have you taken Dr. Nedley's Comprehensive Depression, Anxiety, and EQ Assessment? It is strongly recommended that you do so before continuing. Ask your director or refer to page 19.

Session One
Identifying Depression and Its Causes

DURING this session, pay attention to:

- How most who suffer from depression are never diagnosed.
- Ways to know if it's depression—do any of these apply to you?
- The role genetics and development play in depression.
- What tasks recovery from depression will involve.

You will notice in your workbook that you have the outline of Dr. Nedley's PowerPoint™ presentation for **Session One,** so that you can follow along.

To complete this program successfully you will need:
- *Depression: the Way Out* by Neil Nedley, M.D.
- *SOS: Help for Emotions*–*Managing Anxiety, Anger & Depression* by Lynn Clark, Ph.D.
- *Telling Yourself the Truth: Find Your Way out of Depression, Anxiety, Fear, Anger, and Other Common Problems by Applying the Principles of Misbelief Therapy* by William Backus, Ph.D. and Marie Chapian
- *Feeling Good,* optional.

Learning Styles

Most people seem to learn this material best by taking notes while watching the presentations on one or two blank sheets of paper and then using the "fill in the blank" sections of this workbook as a quiz. However, there are many different learning styles. Understanding this, you should feel free to *use whatever method works best for you* in your journey through this series. Take notes, use the blanks to fill in answers as you go along, or fill the answers in ahead of time using the **Answer Key** at the back of the book.

DVD PowerPoint™ Slides
Session One
Identifying Depression and Its Causes

WHILE watching Dr. Nedley's presentation, follow along with these slides that match those used in the session. If you want to, you can fill in the blanks for the missing words—sometimes a blank equals one word, other times it equals a short phrase. Use the blanks in the margins with letters that correspond to the letters on the blanks on the PowerPoint™ slides to match your answers. (For example, for blank [a] write the answer on the line to the side of the slide marked [a.], and so on.) Answers can be found in the back of this workbook.

1.

DEPRESSION RECOVERY

Identifying Depression and Its Causes

2.

Depression is Increasing

- The number of people developing depression worldwide has steadily increased since ____a____

- Major episodes of depression now occur frequently by age 25. __b__

- Overall risk of depression has increased over time.

a._____

b._____

3.

Impact of Depression

- Affects 350 million people worldwide
- Currently affects more than _____c_____ Americans
- Affects up to 1 in 3 people who see an Internal Medicine physician
- Costs over $70 __d__ dollars in treatment, disability and lost productivity in United States each year

National Institutes of Health and the World Health Organization.

c. _____

d. _____

4.

Lifelong Risk of Depression

- At least _e_ in _f_ women will suffer from major depression at some point in their lives.

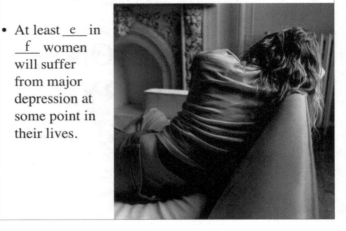

e. _____

f. _____

5.

Lifelong Risk of Depression

- At least _g_ in _h_ men will suffer from major depression at some point in their lives.

g. _____

h. _____

Lifelong Risk of Depression

- 99 percent of people by age 70 will suffer from ___i___ ___j___ at some interval as a result of ___k___ .

6.

i. _____

j. _____

k. _____

Adding to the Sadness

- Most people who suffer from depression are ___l___ .
- Such people never have an opportunity for a ___m___ .
- The condition first needs to be ___n___ .
- Then the ___o___ of the condition needs to be ___p___ .
- Then the cure becomes ___q___ .

7.

l. _____

m. _____

n. _____

o. _____

p. _____

q. _____

How Can I Know if it's Depression?

Cannot have recently faced obvious emotional trauma but still experiences at least 5 of the 9 symptoms for at least 2 weeks.

- Deep sadness
- ___r___
- Agitation
- Sleep disturbances
- Weight or appetite changes
- ___s___

- Feelings of worthlessness
- ___t___
- Fatigue

Subsyndromal Depression = 2 to 4 symptoms for 2 weeks.

8.

r. _____

s. _____

t. _____

27

9.

u. _____

v. _____

w. _____

x. _____

How Can I Know if it's Depression?

- Are you experiencing deep ___u___ or a feeling of ___v___ nearly every day for the past 2 weeks or more?
- Are you experiencing a markedly diminished interest or pleasure in all or nearly all activities for the past 2 ___w___ or more?
- You must have at least one of the above symptoms to qualify as being ___x___.

10.

y. _____

z. _____

a2. _____

Question Number 3

- Have you experienced a ___y___ or ___z___ in ___a2___ ?
  - Or if you weigh 100 pounds, have you gained or lost 5 pounds or more?
  - If you weigh 150 pounds, have you gained or lost 7 pounds or more?
  - If you weigh 200 pounds, have you gained or lost 10 pounds or more?

11.

b2. _____

c2. _____

d2. _____

e2. _____

Question Number 4

- Do you ___b2___ than you used to?
  - To total more than 40 minutes total per day?
  - Or are you more sleepy in the day time and feel like taking nap frequently? (If you are not used to napping.)
- Do you ___c2___ than you used to?
  - To total more than 40 minutes shorter sleep duration?
  - Or difficulty ___d2___ or ___e2___ ?

Question Number 5

- Have you been more _____f2_____ with yourself or others?
- Or you would also qualify for a yes to number 5 if your _____g2_____ have been _h2_ than they used to be?
  - For example have people noticed that you walk slower than you used to?

12.

f2. _____

g2. _____

h2. _____

Question Number 6

- Have you experienced _i2_ ?
- Have you experienced a _____j2_____ ?

13.

i2. _____

j2. _____

Question Number 7

- Have you experienced feelings of _____k2_____ ?
- Have you experienced feelings of ___l2___ or _____m2_____ ?

14.

k2. _____

l2. _____

m2. _____

15.

n2. _____

o2. _____

Question Number 8

- Have you experienced a diminished ability to think or _____n2_____
  - Especially if there is a difficult decision to make
- Do you experience a decrease in your ability to make sound _____o2_____

16.

p2. _____

q2. _____

r2. _____

s2. _____

Question Number 9

- Do you have recurrent _____p2_____
- Or have you seriously contemplated harming _____q2_____
- Have you _____r2_____ considered suicide?
- Have you ____s2____ suicide?

17.

t2. _____

u2. _____

Scoring

- If at least 5 of 9 symptoms are yes, the person is experiencing depression.
- If the person has suffered a _____t2_____ within the last 18 months, then the person is suffering from situational depression or bereavement.
- If the person has not suffered a recent emotional loss, then the person has major depression.
- If only 2 to 4 symptoms are yes, the person has _____u2_____ .

Depression Increases Risk of Death

- Increases risk of __v2__ by 50%
- Increases risk of sudden cardiac death in post-MI survivors by 2½ times
- Increases risk of __w2__ in men
- Increases risk of death from cancer
- Increases risk of death from pneumonia
- Increases __x2__

Journal of Epidemiology. 1997;7:210-213.
British Medical Journal. 1998;316:1714-1719.

18.

v2. _____

w2. _____

x2. _____

Effects of Depression

- May cause a chronic __y2__
- May cause __z2__
- When combined with stress, increases risk of HIV progressing to AIDS
- Increases risk of return to __a3__ such as drinking
- May increase problems with __b3__

Archives of General Psychiatry. 1998;55:259-265.
American Journal of Psychiatry. 1997; 154(5):630-634.
The Journal of the American Medical Association. 1998; 279:1720-1726.

19.

y2. _____

z2. _____

a3. _____

b3. _____

Effects of Depression

- Increases risk of developing __c3__
- Increases chance that __d3__ will suffer depression and physical medical problems
- Increases rate of decline in physical abilities with age
- Increases stress hormones
- Decreases __e3__
- Decreases CD8, Increases IgA, Decreases IgM, impairing immune system
- Decreases __f3__

Archives of General Psychiatry. 1998;55:259-265.
American Journal of Psychiatry. 1997; 154(5):630-634.
The Journal of the American Medical Association. 1998; 279:1720-1726.

20.

c3. _____

d3. _____

e3. _____

f3. _____

21.

g3. _____

h3. _____

i3. _____

j3. _____

k3. _____

l3. _____

Major Depression--constellation of symptoms

- The ___g3___ does not give any indication to the ___h3___ of the disease.
- If we want to increase the likelihood of a long term solution, we will ___i3___ of depression and ___j3___ treat them.
- Unfortunately this is not as simple a process as ___k3___ .
- Like most chronic diseases, depression is a multifactorial disease.
- The most effective treatments will be based on an ___l3___ on as many causes identified to be operative.

22.

The Ten "Hit" Categories

1. Genetic
2. Developmental
3. Lifestyle
4. Circadian Rhythm
5. Addiction

6. Nutrition
7. Toxic
8. Social/Complicated Stress or Grief
9. Medical Condition
10. Frontal Lobe

23.

m3. _____

n3. _____

o3. _____

1. The Genetic Hit

- ___m3___ for depression
- Family history of depression in ___n3___ relative
  - Increases likelihood 1.5 to 3 times
- ___o3___ in future

British Medical Journal. 1998;316:1-5. Journal of the American Academy of Child and Adolescent Psychiatry. 1998;37:473-487. J Am Acad Child Adolesc Psychiatry. 1997;36:255-262. J Am Acad Child Adolesc Psychiatry. 1996;35(12):1602-1610. Archives of General Psychiatry. 1998;55:161-166. Arch General Psychiatry. 1997;54:124-130. Molecular Psychiatry. 1998;3:86-91. Archives of Family Medicine. 1997;6:445-452.

2. The Developmental Hit

- Not being raised by _____p3_____
- History of depression in adolescence
- Severe ____q3____
- History of alcohol or illicit drug use as teen
- ____r3____ Development

24.

p3. _____

q3. _____

r3. _____

The Set-up

- Early ____s3____ in girls
- Girls who, by age 11 or younger, are at the middle of their puberty phase of development have ___t3___ the risk of developing depressed symptoms in their teenage years and into adulthood.
- The risk of developing _____u3_____ in these girls is also increased.

25.

s3. _____

t3. _____

u3. _____

It's the Protein

- Japanese fare is characterized by a ____v3____ diet and is associated with an average age of menstruation of 17.
- Here, in the U.S. with our ____w3____ diet, that age is as low as 12.
- Recent study of 67 white females in the United States
- The higher the ____x3____ intake at ages three to five, the earlier the first ____y3____ .
- Girls that consumed higher amounts of ____z3____ protein at ages three to five had a ____a4____ of menstruation.

Catherine S. Berkey American Journal of Epidemiology 2000;152:446-452

26.

v3. _____

w3. _____

x3. _____

y3. _____

z3. _____

a4. _____

27.

Bad News—Good News

- Bad news—there isn't much we can do about our genes or our development.
  - Although we can do something, if informed early enough, about our children's and grandchildren's development
- Good News—the other 8 hits we can modify in most cases so that depression can be cured in 5 months or less—even if our genes and upbringing was flawed.

28.

b4. _____

c4. _____

d4. _____

The Twenty Week Cure
(The Twenty Week Turn Around)

- Work on all of the ___b4___ causes under a given hit category at one time.
- Work on all ___c4___ in a hit category at one time
- Zero hit categories ideal but not absolutely necessary
- Withdrawal ___d4___ under doctor's supervision

29.

e4. _____

Depression Recovery

- 90 percent success rate in ___e4___ to the program
- Such patients often feel better than they have felt their entire lives
  - Getting more done
  - More efficient
  - Social problems vanish
  - Able to concentrate and accomplish advanced planning and thinking

Will Involve

- Learning More About ____f4____
- Making ____g4____
- Building ____h4____

30.

f4. _____

g4. _____

h4. _____

Get Ready For

- Happiness
- ____i4____
- Better Decisions
- ____j4____
- ____k4____ in Life

31.

i4. _____

j4. _____

k4. _____

ೞ

What You Learned

- Both men and women have a significant chance of suffering from major depression at some time in their lives.
- Depression is a constellation of symptoms.
- The effects of depression increase the risk of many diseases and premature death.
- Genetics and development both play a role in depression.
- Once the underlying causes are determined, a cure can be found.

છ

Daily Dose

> *Reading Prescriptions* elaborate on what you have just learned. They come at the end of each session, and are meant to be read during the week before the next session meets.

Reading Prescription
- *Depression: the Way Out*, Chapter One: The Marvelous Mind and the Invisible Disease, pages 1–12, and Chapter Two: Depression's Hidden Dangers, pages 13–30.
- *Depression: the Way Out*: Chapter Three: What Causes Depression?, pages 31–59, and Chapter Ten: The Twenty Week Turn Around.
- Chapter of Proverbs (from the Bible) that corresponds with today's date. (Example: July 31, read Proverbs 31.)
- *SOS: Help for Emotions–Managing Anxiety, Anger & Depression* by Lynn Clark, Ph.D. Begin reading, and continue reading at your own pace, but as quickly as you can.

Lifestyle Matters

1. Accentuate the Positive, Eliminate the Negative

What we converse about can influence the positive or negative direction of our health. The following exercise will greatly benefit you if you dedicate yourself to succeeding.

For two weeks, 14 consecutive days, decide to say nothing critical or negative about anything or any person (refer to page 50). In this exercise, not one critical word is allowed to be spoken to others (not even "constructive" criticism). This may seem impossible for those raising children or leading others in a business environment, but realize that expectations and consequences can still be enforced without critical words.

Speak to others using positive words and thoughts or speak nothing at all! If you slip up on any day during the two weeks, you must begin counting again until you achieve all 14 consecutive days. Don't get discouraged if you have to start over; it gets easier as you become more aware of your thoughts. Remember, this program is eight weeks long! Virtually everyone will be able to do it by week eight.

Quotes to Encourage You:

- "Nothing tends more to promote health of body and of soul than does a spirit of gratitude."
  — "Mind Cure" in *The Ministry of Healing*, page 251.

- "Cultivate the habit of thankfulness. Praise God over and over again for His wonderful love in giving Christ to die for us. It never pays to think of old grievances. God calls upon us to cultivate His mercy and His matchless love, that we may be inspired with praise."
  —"True Worship" in *Bible Training School*, page 1.

2. Keep Your Mind in Tune

We could call this "music therapy." Classical music has been scientifically shown to improve mood, calm nerves, and improve the function of our brains. This benefits all forms of depression. Though you may not be familiar with or even enjoy classical music at this time, this activity is nonetheless effective and important. Listening intently to classical music no less than one hour every two weeks will help lift your mood and establish good mental clarity.

While listening, pay attention to the music and reflect upon your life. Thinking about how you would like your future to be different from your past, or just taking stock of the good things and relationships in your life can be excellent examples. Listening to classical music while driving or writing out "to do" lists—although probably helpful—does *not* count as time towards this exercise. The only requirement is that you must think about areas of concern in your life and keep your mind and imagination active during the music.

Remember to listen to classical music daily as well—while driving, cleaning house, at the office, at live concerts, and church hymns.

It is important to note that not every type of music can qualify for this activity. The classical music you select should be more traditional and less experimental or strange. Albinoni, Bach, Beethoven, Brahms, Handel, Mozart, Respighi, Ravel, Tchaikovsky and Vivaldi are but a few of the composers you can choose from. Also remember that as you begin this regular exercise of the mind, it is not important that you like classical music. You will benefit from it regardless of your tastes in music, and you will find it more enjoyable over time. Dr. Nedley's Health Solutions carries a variety of classical music CDs—to place an order, call the toll-free number listed on the back of this workbook or the DVD case.

3. The Water of Life

The brain and body both need significant hydration to function well. So, consider the implications of *not* getting enough water each day.

Our blood is also greatly affected by not getting enough water. It circulates through the body and brain a lot better when it's not so thick and sluggish. All this adds up to better overall body and brain health.

Drink large quantities of fresh, pure water between your meals each day. And "water substitutes" don't count; colas and other soft drinks, coffee and tea, and even juices are not good enough. In fact, many water substitutes will actually increase our need for more water each day. Drink eight full eight-ounce glasses of water each day starting today. And while in the heat or during physical work or exercise you need to consume more water to keep up with the loss.

Tips for Success: Each day, set out your eight glasses and fill them with water. Or if you care to use water bottles, get multiple bottles, measure out the proper amount, and set them where you will be throughout the day to make it easy. You can also set yourself goals like one to three glasses before breakfast, lunch, and dinner so that you get them all finished by the end of the day.

4. Mind Your Body, Better Your Mind

Many people who have not previously used exercise as a fitness tool are afraid to start. There are legitimate concerns, and inactive people over 35 need to check with their physician before beginning an exercise program to make sure they don't aggravate a heart condition or other physical illness.

Exercise can take many forms, but as long as it gets your body moving and your blood pumping, it will benefit your depression. A good way to track the number of steps you take (and the distance you travel) in a day is to use a device intended for this purpose, called a pedometer (check with your facilitator to obtain one.)

Begin your exercise program this week—twice daily, for 30 to 60 minutes a session.

1. The best way to get started with exercise is to start a walking program.
2. Before stepping out, warm up to increase blood flow to the muscles and joints.
3. Once you are in good enough shape, move on to more vigorous aerobic activities, such as these listed below:
     A.   Bicycling
     B.   Jogging
     C.   Brisk walking (try actively swinging your arms, too)
     D.   Tennis or racquetball
     E.   Swimming
     F.   Ice or roller skating or rollerblading (inline skating)
     G.   Cross-country skiing
     H.   Aerobics
     I.   Vigorous gardening

Raising your heart rate will help you to process a large amount of oxygen, increasing your energy level, and helping you to feel great.

The sing-talk test is a good way to test if you are exercising too hard or not enough. Here's an easy way to tell—if you can't talk while exercising, you're working too hard. If you can sing, step up the pace a little.

Remember: Stay committed and keep exercising.

Keeping on Track: Using the Healthy Lifestyle Scorecard

The **Healthy Lifestyle Scorecard** (see page 41) includes eight categories that are important to your recovery: Exercise, Sleep, Deep Breathing, Avoiding Negative Speech, Water, Spiritual Activity, Classical Music, and Sunlight. A copy of the Healthy Lifestyle

> USE THE HEALTHY LIFESTYLE SCORECARD to keep track of how you're doing on the different parts of the *Depression Recovery Program.* You can write your answers here in the book, copy or photocopy it onto another sheet, or use a dry-erase board if that is easier for you. The success rate of this program is higher with those who comply with filling in the scorecard.

Scorecard appears at the end of each chapter of this workbook.

For each day of the week, you need to keep an account of the amount of time spent (or in the case of water, how many total ounces you consumed) and, perhaps even more importantly, the time of day when you did the activity.

For example, the first activity on the scorecard is "Exercise." You should take note of when you began and ended your exercise, for example, by writing "8:10 – 8:42 AM" in the space provided. If you spread your exercise out over several sessions throughout the day, record those times as well, according to the beginning and end of the activity. At the end of the day, write a total in the box for how many minutes you exercised. Follow this pattern for the rest of the score card as well.

Here is an example:
• Sleep: 9 – 11 PM, awake again from 1 – 4 AM, asleep from 4–7 AM (awake for the day)

The **spaces** on the **Healthy Lifestyle Scorecard** may be too **small** for you to easily record this much information, so feel free to write the categories and detailed information on a **separate sheet of paper and keep it with the scorecard.**

Healthy Lifestyle Scorecard Week __

Day	Sun	Mon	Tues	Wed	Thur	Fri	Sat
Date							
Exercise *Beginning and ending times for exercise sessions.*							
Sleep *Beginning and ending times for sleep.*							
Deep Breathing *Beginning and ending times for when you practiced deep breathing.*							
Avoided Negative Speech *Beginning and ending times for when you avoided negative speech.*							
Water *How many ounces of water you drank in a day, along with the times of day.*							
Spiritual Activity *Daily time reading Proverbs and praying. Also, write what time(s).*							
Favorite Verse							
Classical Music *Beginning and ending times for when you listened to classical music.*							
Sunlight *Beginning and ending times for sunlight or lightbox use.*							

Session Two
Lifestyle Treatment for Depression

DURING this session, pay attention to:

- What we can and cannot **change** about ourselves.
- How **Intermittent Training (IT)** can help you become fit more quickly.
- Why depressed individuals benefit from **deep breathing.**
- The importance of **avoiding pessimism** and **dwelling on the good.**

Your *Workbook* contains the slides from Dr. Nedley's PowerPoint™ presentation for **Session Two.** Please follow along as you watch the DVD.

DVD PowerPoint™ Slides
Session Two
Lifestyle Treatment for Depression

WHILE watching Dr. Nedley's presentation, follow along with these slides that match those used in the session. If you want to, you can fill in the blanks for the missing words—sometimes a blank equals one word, other times it equals a short phrase. Use the blanks in the margins with letters that correspond to the letters on the blanks on the PowerPoint™ slides to match your answers. (For example, for blank [a] write the answer on the line to the side of the slide marked [a.], and so on.) Answers can be found in the back of this workbook.

1.

DEPRESSION RECOVERY

Lifestyle Treatment for Depression

2.

Major Depression--constellation of symptoms

3.

The Ten "Hit" Categories

1. Genetic
2. Developmental
3. Lifestyle
4. Circadian rhythm
5. Addiction
6. Nutrition
7. Toxic
8. Social/Complicated Grief
9. Medical Condition
10. Frontal Lobe

4.

Bad News—Good News

- Bad news—there isn't much we can do about our genes or our development.
  - Although we can do something, if informed early enough, about our children's and grandchildren's development
- Good News—the other 8 hits we can modify in most cases so that depression can be cured in 5 months or less—even if our genes and upbringing was flawed.

5.

3. Lifestyle Hits

- Not on a regular _____ a _____
- Not regularly being exposed to daylight at least _____ b _____
- Rarely _____ c _____

a. _____

b. _____

c. _____

d. _____

e. _____

f. _____

6.

Taking Long Walks

- _____d_____ Does Not Have to Involve Elaborate Equipment
- Taking _____e_____ are very beneficial in reducing depression
- Hour long walks are the best
- _____f_____ for positive results in most cases

g. _____

h. _____

i. _____

7.

Becoming Fit through Exercise

- _____g_____ (or I.T.)
- Mixes Rest with Exercise
- Accelerates fitness to a high level in a shorter time period
- Ideal for both the __h__ and the __i__
- No muscle soreness
- Thyroid function significantly improves

j. _____

k. _____

l. _____

8.

Intermittent Training

- Exercise vigorously to achieve desired __j__ rate
- When heart rate goes to the upper limit, then __k__
- When heart rate drops to the lower limit, then ___l___ vigorous exercise

Got to "Force" Yourself at First

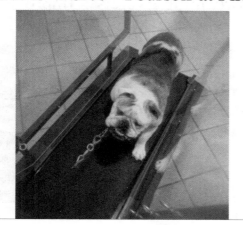

9.

Bright Light Therapy

- Light needed for adequate ___m___ production
- Possibly best within 10 minutes after ___n___
- Works best for those that also are fatigued or have disordered sleep, or winter depression.
- Effective for _____o_____ depression
- 10,000 lux light boxes 30-60 minutes/day, or 2500 lux light boxes 1-2 hours/day.

10.

m. _____

n. _____

o. _____

Exercise Outdoors in Daylight

11.

12.

p. _____

q. _____

r. _____

s. _____

Breathing Exercises Improve Mood

Low blood oxygen levels
 – Impairs __p__ Function
 – Impairs __q__ Function
 – Leads to Muscle __r__
 – Leads to Exercise __s__

Bernardi, Luciano. Lancet 1998;351: 1308-1311

13.

t. _____

u. _____

Breathing Exercises Improve Fitness

Breathing exercises encouraging slow deep breathing of 6 breaths per minute for one hour a day improves _____t_____ levels through out the day and improves exercise tolerance in cardiac patients. This improvement is __u__ to other forms of treatment.

Bernardi, Luciano. Lancet 1998;351: 1308-1311

14.

v. _____

w. _____

x. _____

4. Circadian Rhythm Hits

- _____v_____
- Sleeping more than 9 hours a day routinely
- Sleeping less than 6 hours a day routinely
- "Shift" Work
- Not having regular hours for __w__ and __x__

Depression and Insomnia

- Ironically, the depression seems to __y__ and the energy level ___z___ as the person stays awake.
- Going to bed late or "sleep deprivation" is a temporary treatment for "circadian rhythm" depression.

- Once sleep occurs, the depression ___a2___ causing the person to not want to get up or be a ___b2___ in the morning.

15.

y. _____

z. _____

a2. _____

b2. _____

Treatment

- _____c2_____ , or be exposed to at least 30 minutes of bright light starting within ___d2___ of awakening.
- Regular hours for sleeping, eating, and exercise.
- Requires an alarm clock at first.
- Sleep's Three Factor
  - ___e2___
  - ___f2___
  - ___g2___

16.

c2. _____

d2. _____

e2. _____

f2. _____

g2. _____

Avoid Pessimism

224 subjects were studied as to their degree of optimism and pessimism.

Pessimism Predicted:
  - ___h2___
  - ___i2___
  - Physical Disease

Optimism Predicted ___j2___

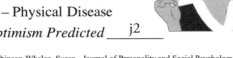
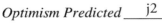

Robinson-Whelen, Susan. Journal of Personality and Social Psychology. 1997;73:1345-1353.

17.

h2. _____

i2. _____

j2. _____

18.

k2. _____

Avoid Pessimism

"While the 'power of positive thinking' is encouraged as a way to improve health and well being, this study shows it is more important to
_____ k2 _____ ."

Robinson-Whelen, Susan. Journal of Personality and Social Psychology. 1997;73:1345-1353.

19.

l2. _____

m2. _____

Dwell on the Good

- Avoid pessimism
- Not permitted to say anything critical about anyone or anything for 14 consecutive days (2 weeks).
- Once _____ l2 _____ is said, begin the 14 days ___ m2 ___ .

20.

n2. _____

o2. _____

p2. _____

The Top Priority in Healthful Living

"Nothing tends more to promote _____ n2 _____ and of soul than does a spirit of ___ o2 ___ and ___ p2 ___ ."

MH 251

21.

Take Control of Your Life
- By improving your _____q2_____

q2. _____

&cx;

What You Learned

- Intermittent Training is a proven way to accelerate physical fitness.
- Breathing exercises can improve health and aid mental clarity.
- Early morning sunlight is best for improving mood.
- You can take control of your life by improving your lifestyle.
- An attitude of gratitude is of great benefit to you.

&cx;

Daily Dose

Reading Prescription
- *Depression: the Way Out*: Chapter 5: Lifestyle Treatments for Depression, pages 79–95.
- *Telling Yourself the Truth* chapters 1–3.
- Chapter of Proverbs (from the Bible) that corresponds with today's date. (Example: July 31, read Proverbs 31.)
- *SOS: Help for Emotions* – chapters 4, 5, 6.

Lifestyle Matters

1. Breath of Life

Scientific studies show that when the oxygen levels in the body (especially blood and brain) are lower than optimum, the mood is dramatically affected. Pure air improves muscle function, mental power, and exercise tolerance. It is important to keep your oxygen levels high.

One very effective way to accomplish this is through deep breathing exercises. Ideal oxygen levels are reached during deep breathing at three to six breaths per minute. To prevent shortness of breath while breathing six times per minute it is necessary to breathe very deeply. This not only improves blood oxygen levels during the time of exercise but throughout the entire day!

This week start your deep breathing program by standing or sitting with erect, proper posture and taking very deep breaths using a watch with a second hand. Time yourself as you inhale slowly and deeply for five seconds. Then exhale slowly for five seconds. Focus on the air going in and out when you inhale and exhale. Breathe into the bottom part of your lungs (your upper lungs and chest will fill up automatically.) Your belly should expand as you breathe in and contract as you breathe out. Your goal is to spend 30 to 45 minutes each day taking no more than six complete breaths each minute. You will notice tremendous benefits! Divide the time into two or three sessions if you need to, but be sure to get the total time each day.

2. Light Up Your Life

Seasonal Affective Disorder (SAD) mimics depression's symptoms, but can be easily remedied. Daily exposure to bright light for at least 30 minutes allows our open eyes to receive sufficiently intense light (2,000 to 10,000 lux) which helps our brain and body produce important neurotransmitter chemicals. These tiny substances help our brain and moods keep in proper balance. Sufficient bright light exposure is therefore critical for all those suffering from depression.

Bright light therapy can also help restore the normal daily body rhythm called circadian rhythm. If a person has a difficult time getting up in the morning or considers himself to be a night person, chances are very good that there is a problem with the circadian rhythm. This can be corrected by getting 30 minutes of daily exposure to bright light within 10 minutes of awakening. Outdoor daylight is approximately 15 times brighter than normal indoor lighting. So if you cannot enjoy daylight first thing upon awakening due to schedule or environment, it will be necessary to purchase a light therapy box with a rating of 10,000 lux. These boxes vary in terms of the distance one must be from the light source for effective therapy—some may need to be held near your face; others are intended for use within 16 to 24 inches. There are many companies that sell light therapy boxes through the Internet and mail order. Check www.drnedley.com for one option. Alternately, you can check a local medical supply company, pharmacy, or health food store. Insomnia or unwanted early morning awakening (for instance 1:30 or 2:30 AM) can be corrected by bright light exposure for 30 minutes in mid-to-late afternoon.

This week you must get outdoor light (or bright light therapy box) exposure for at least 30 minutes per day.

    a. What time have you set as your wake up time? _____

    b. When will you get your bright light therapy? _____

Tips for Success: You can combine bright light therapy with outdoor exercise, reading, or listening to classical music. For instance, walking outdoors while listening to classical music on headphones, or indoors reading in front of your lightbox.

3. Get in Touch with Massage

The greatest value of massage is in its action on the circulatory system.[1] The amount of stress and tension created by modern lifestyles and schedules cause increased tension in the muscles of the upper back and neck. As a result, pain and headaches may occur, affecting mental performance. Massage combined with other treatments can be used profitably in nervous and emotional disorders.[2] In order for a massage to be most effective, it should take about an hour. However, even a moment of massage can do a small amount of good.[1]

Although the exact mechanism is not known, therapeutic massage is beneficial for a variety of ailments by promoting relaxation. Physiological measures such as heart rate, respiratory rate and blood pressure decrease from baseline during massage, providing further evidence of its relaxing properties.

Good massages teach relaxation in general, as well. Through awareness of muscle tension, posture can improve. Imagine a forward-leaning, stooped posture being corrected. A new, erect back posture increases the rib cage size, so lung capacity is increased and more air is exchanged. This in turn increases the amount of oxygen carried by the vessels to the brain, so that frontal lobe function may be enhanced.

[1] Thrash, Agatha and Calvin. *Home Remedies.* Thrash Publications, Seale, Alabama, 1981.
[2] The Physician and Sportsmedicine 8(12):25, Dec 1980

4. Stimulating Contrast Showers

Hydrotherapy, the therapeutic use of water, has been used successfully for centuries for a number of physical and mental ailments. One way of using hydrotherapy to stimulate the body's circulatory and nervous system involves alternating hot and cold water in the shower.

When using this method of treatment, the same precautions should be observed as when preparing for a vigorous exercise program; a recent physical examination from your physician is advised in order to be certain that you are healthy enough to engage in this activity. **Persons with heart disease, blood pressure problems, or other serious health conditions should not use contrast showers.**

The following steps will guide you in using this therapy:

While in the shower, gradually adjust the temperature to as warm as your skin will allow and stay under the water for four to five minutes. Then turn the faucet all the way to cold while vigorously rinsing your entire body for thirty seconds. This is one cycle. Next, turn the water back to hot and stand and stay under the water for one to two minutes. Repeat this process until you have completed three rounds of hot water and three rounds of cold water, finishing with cold water. This is breathtaking—but refreshing. (Hint: take a timer and place it in a water-tight plastic bag so that you can take it with you into the shower to time your hot-cold cycles.)

Next, dry off and dress for sleep. Rest in bed for a minimum of thirty minutes making sure to keep warm and comfortable. This is a very important step! Do not miss this portion! Your body has been through severe stimulation and needs the rest to properly benefit from the treatment. The resting should be done especially during the first week. After that, you will find the shower exhilarating and will not need to rest afterward.

For those who are severely depressed, this treatment must be done two times a day for seven to ten days. Once the depression is mild, decrease the treatment to once each day. When no depression is present, three treatments per week should be done for at least six months.

The application of hot and cold to relieve depressive symptoms is so effective—so safe and easy—and free from bad side effects and expense that it can be done frequently.

> **Note:** The hottest water should not exceed 104° Fahrenheit. Your water heater has a control that allows you to adjust it so that it will not exceed the set temperature. Before doing this treatment, you can check the maximum temperature that your shower will reach by adjusting the faucet so that only hot water is flowing, measuring it with a thermometer. This will help you to avoid scalding yourself, and aid in peace of mind by knowing that the water will not be dangerously hot. The cold water should be no colder than 55° F.

5. Continue Your Exercise Program

Like with any lifestyle change, you may not notice any significant benefits or improvement in your depression within one week. Remember, even antidepressant medications can take up to two weeks to notice a difference. Stay with your positive new exercise routine consistently and *improvement will come.*

a. Are you exercising 30 minutes to one hour per day at least five days per week?   yes   no

b. If yes, keep up the good work and don't let *anything* interrupt your new healthy habit.

c. If no, think about why you are not accomplishing this important goal. Almost any excuse you can raise has a solution if you are determined to get and stay well. Review the possible exercise choices in Session One's Lifestyle Matters section and select at least one you will do this week. Write it here: _____

Tips for Success: Introduce a new sport or exercise into your routine, or listen to classical music as you exercise. Changing it up, if you are able, will keep freshness and excitement in your life. If you live in a climate that makes it difficult to exercise outdoors part of the year, many indoor shopping malls encourage walkers. Another option is an aerobic exercise video. Remember, there's no such thing as "bad weather," only "bad clothing."

Is disability threatening to keep you from exercising? Talk with someone familiar with exercise (for example: a trainer at a gym, YMCA, or community center) who can suggest a routine which works with your limitations. Remember, you want to get well and exercise is a vital key to your wellness.

Walking is a great exercise, but walking without warming up your muscles isn't so great—you run a greater risk of strain. You can do ankle circles, leg swings, or start out walking slowly. After walking for three to five minutes, you are already warmed up, so you can safely pick up your pace. Remember, stretch again after you finish walking. Also remember to measure your steps and distance with a pedometer.

Intermittent Training (I.T.)
You Can Do I.T.!

Most complaints raised by newcomers to exercise center on their fear of muscle soreness and difficulty breathing.

The fact is, when done right, exercise can be an enjoyable way to increase our quality of life and mood. There are so many different things that qualify as "exercise" that you can easily incorporate energy and excitement into getting started. Pick some types that work well with your schedule, ability, and physical aptitude. With a proper understanding of I.T., we can realize that the old saying, "No pain, no gain," is completely *false*.

Exercise should not be "all work and no play" or "all work and no rest." I.T. helps incorporate rest as a natural part of exercise. Just as the heart muscle shows the benefits of alternating activity with rest, I.T. teaches that rest makes the work more effective. It's how our muscles and bodies were made to get the most out of life. It's the excellent choice for those who are unfit or who want to get more out of their exercise minutes without muscle soreness.

Most people think they would get more out of their exercise if they could push themselves harder and longer until they are completely exhausted. But scientific research shows that by adding a portion of rest into every minute of our exercise, we more efficiently build up our muscles and cardiovascular fitness. We get more for less!

Here's how you can get started with I.T. Begin with 5 to 10 minutes of gentle stretching. Next, warm up your circulatory system with 5 minutes of slow, comfortable walking at a continuous pace. Now you're ready to begin the exercise of your choice I.T. style. At a vigorous pace, do the exercise of your choice for 60 seconds. Once this is achieved, it's time for a rest. But don't stop completely; instead slow down to a gentle, easy pace until your heart rate slows slightly. Usually 30 seconds is enough. Then begin your vigorous pace again for the next interval of 60 seconds and rest again. Eventually, your intervals of exercise and rest will change as you improve (e.g., 5 minutes exercise, 30 seconds rest).

Continue alternating between very active then milder exercise intervals until your total time is achieved. You've done I.T.! Once you've finished, it's a good idea to take 5 to 10 minutes for "cool down," so do some more gentle stretching and slow, comfortable walking to finish up. Entire books have been written on this subject, but these are the basics. You'll be much more inclined to exercise tomorrow if you didn't hurt yourself with today's program, so try I.T.

A Testimony to Reflect Upon

Dear Dr. Nedley,

I thought you might like to hear my wonderful story of deliverance!

I didn't know I was depressed. My husband thought my hormones had gone haywire and pleaded for years for me to see a doctor, which I did without any positive results. All I knew was that I married the wrong man and, being a Christian, was not able to divorce. There was a bigger picture that included my children, my husband's job as a pastor, and all my friends who often commented about our "good marriage." Boy, could I fake it! But inside...

I was so angry and being eaten alive by negative thoughts. My thoughts were fearful and I could imagine all the horrors of the last days. During certain times of the month I would pick on my husband incessantly. I really didn't like most everyone but he was the one that got the brunt of all the pent up anger and frustration. My thoughts were extreme and fanatical. I thought everyone else was a poor example of a Christian. I felt very much alone, very alone.

One day while watching Three Angels Broadcasting Network (3ABN) my husband heard of tryptophan from a physician. I called a doctor and he suggested I start taking 100 mg. three times a day. After just a few weeks I thought I was feeling considerably better. Oh, I was still angry, still had some mood swings, but not so severe. I took tryptophan as a supplement for about three years, trying to get off of it about every six to eight months. Each time I would announce, "I am cured! I'm getting off the tryptophan!" My children would plead, "Mom, please take a vacation while you do that!" In reality I would have loved to take a vacation and get away from them all. I needed lots of time without someone trying my patience (easy to do). I was an emotion-stuffer, and my net was crammed, but not breaking loose. I thought that was the best I could hope for.

My husband was still telling me my hormones were messed up. I got a book on hormones and started taking them. That helped a bit in some areas, but I still didn't have peace, real peace, deep in my heart. I thought that Christ was going to keep self-hidden (not dead) and I could wear his robe to cover up the inner pain.

I was beginning to realize my life was out of control. I had had stomach problems for years and continual thoughts of running away. It was sort of frightening at times.

Then I got *Depression: the Way Out*. I read that tryptophan supplements could have side effects. That just about gave me an anxiety attack! How could I live without it? While reading the book, I would try this or that, not with tremendous results. For instance, I thought light therapy could be attained with "Reveal" light bulbs. So I got lots of those. I was already in the habit of regular devotional time each morning, ate a vegan diet sprinkled with walnuts or flax and did a few other little things, but I hadn't "arrived."

In desperation I nervously and tearfully called Dr. Nedley's office. The woman was helpful and very to the point. "You've got to do it ALL." She ran through the list of "to do's" that were all in the book (many I had overlooked). It was an almost overwhelming list! It seemed like I had something serious like cancer; this was intense! I began to realize that what I had was as serious as cancer because it was killing my family. But NO critical words for 14 days or start counting over again?! Seemed impossible! But I had run out of vain solutions.

I posted little sticky notes with "14" all over the house to remind me of my countdown. One week later, I had walls dotted with "14"s. I was feeling a bit discouraged. Was I really that wretched? After about a week or two I really let my husband have it. He said I needed to get some professional help and stop trying to self-treat. Within the next day or two a TREMENDOUS light went on. I have not been the same since.

I am free. I feel like a new person. My walk with God is sweeter than ever and my marriage is delightful, and so is my husband. I think he's a new man! But honestly, he hasn't changed, it is my heart that has changed. My children are more affectionate and my daughter says I'm so easy to get along with. And best of all, I feel like I have the mind of Christ. The judgmental, fearful, hateful thoughts are 98% gone and when I feel tensions arise, I think, this is a strange thought and through knowledge or prayer can conquer and expel it as quickly as it came.

What seemed like extreme therapeutic efforts are, in reality, not that hard at all. It was worth every minute spent. I want to continue with all the "steps" for the results cannot be explained; like being born again, it must be experienced to be believed. I'm down to one tryptophan a day, and am confident I will be totally off it very soon.

The last six weeks have been the best in 20 years. I hadn't had six consecutive good days in 20 years, or hardly six consecutive hours of peaceful thoughts. I am completely serious. Praise God for His power to heal. I thank you, Dr. Nedley, for your work. Thank God for my patient family that has loved me all these years.

I can now look forward to the next 20 years of marriage to the wonderful man God has given me, my beautiful children, and the precious church families whom we are blessed to serve. I need to sign off before I cry for complete joy. My heart is full.

Blessings to you, Dr. Nedley. May the Lord grant you strength and wisdom to order your steps and continue to point people in the way of healing.

"He brought me up also out of an horrible pit, out of the miry clay, and set my feet upon a rock, and established my goings. And he hath put a new song in my mouth, even praise unto our God." Psalm 40:2–3

Joyfully His,
Leslie

PS— I now love classical music!

Healthy Lifestyle Scorecard   **Week** ___

Day	Sun	Mon	Tues	Wed	Thur	Fri	Sat
Date							
Exercise *Beginning and ending times for exercise sessions.*							
Sleep *Beginning and ending times for sleep.*							
Deep Breathing *Beginning and ending times for when you practiced deep breathing.*							
Avoided Negative Speech *Beginning and ending times for when you avoided negative speech.*							
Water *How many ounces of water you drank in a day, along with the times of day.*							
Spiritual Activity *Daily time reading Proverbs and praying. Also, write what time(s).*							
Favorite Verse							
Classical Music *Beginning and ending times for when you listened to classical music.*							
Sunlight *Beginning and ending times for sunlight or lightbox use.*							

Session Three
Nutrition and the Brain

DURING this session, pay attention to:

- The clues of a nutrition hit.
- Benefits associated with adequate omega-3 intake.
- Secrets of healthy weight loss and risks of obesity.
- Herbs that can sometimes help improve well-being.

Your *Workbook* contains the slides from Dr. Nedley's PowerPoint™ presentation for **Session Three.** Please follow along as you watch the DVD.

DVD PowerPoint™ Slides
Session Three
Nutrition and the Brain

WHILE watching Dr. Nedley's presentation, follow along with these slides that match those used in the session. If you want to, you can fill in the blanks for the missing words—sometimes a blank equals one word, other times it equals a short phrase. Use the blanks in the margins with letters that correspond to the letters on the blanks on the PowerPoint™ slides to match your answers. (For example, for blank [a] write the answer on the line to the side of the slide marked [a.], and so on.) Answers can be found in the back of this workbook.

1.

DEPRESSION RECOVERY

Nutrition and the Brain

2.

Major Depression--constellation
of symptoms

3.

The Ten "Hit" Categories

1. Genetic
2. Developmental
3. Lifestyle
4. Circadian rhythm
5. Addiction
6. Nutrition
7. Toxic
8. Social/Complicated Grief
9. Medical Condition
10. Frontal Lobe

4.

6. Nutrition Hits

- Possibly the most _____a_____ of depression
- Can have profound effects
- Once a _____b_____ adopted, takes 7 to 10 days to begin noticing a difference
- Gradual improvement continues
- Peaks at _____c_____

a. _____

b. _____

c. _____

5.

Clues of a "Nutrition Hit"

- Dietary Inventory indicates a lot of junk food and/or meat
- Signs of a _____d_____ addict
  - Sugar temporarily increases brain serotonin levels, helping the person "feel better."
- Low serum B-12 or folate
- Often no _____e_____ are present

d. _____

e. _____

6.

Foods Rich in _____f_____

(mg/100 grams)

Whole milk	46
Blackeyed Cowpeas	267
Black Walnuts	290
Almonds	322
Sesame Seeds	358
Gluten flour	510
Roasted pumpkin seeds	578
Tofu	747

0   100   200   300   400   500   600   700   800

f. _____

7.

Nutritional Causes of Depression

- Insufficient dietary _____g_____
- Low _____h_____ intake

g. _____

h. _____

Nature Medicine. 1997;4(7):25-30. The Lancet. 1997;349:915-919.
Journal of Clinical Psychiatry. 1998;154(4):497-501.
Am. J. Psychiatry. 1997;154:426-428. Nature. 1997;386:824-827

8.

_____i_____ Supplements Help _____j_____ Depression

Patients receiving omega 3 supplements "had a significantly longer period of remission (from illness) than the placebo group." Patients receiving omega 3 supplements also displayed considerable improvement on tests assessing levels of depression and other bipolar symptoms.

In an editorial, Dr. Joseph Calabrese and colleagues at Case Western Reserve University in Cleveland, Ohio, call the trial a "landmark attempt in drug development for bipolar disorder."

Archives of General Psychiatry 1999;56:407-412, 413-414, 415-416

i. _____

j. _____

9.

Plant Foods Containing ___k___ (Linolenic Acid)

Food Item	Amount	Omega-3 (mg)
Flaxseed/Linseed oil	1 Tbs.	7526
Flax seeds, ground	2 Tbs.	4350
Walnuts, English	¼ cup	1703
Walnuts, black	¼ cup	1034
Wheat germ oil	1 Tbs.	938
Soybean oil (Crisco/Wesson)	1 Tbs.	927
Tofu, raw	8 oz.	720
Green soybeans	1 cup	637
Spinach canned	1 cup	353
Wheat germ, toasted	2 Tbs.	190
Almonds	¼ cup	136

k. _____

10.

FLAX-NUT SPRINKLE RECIPE

- ¼ cup _____l_____
- ¼ cup flax meal
- 1 tablespoon date sugar _____m_____
- 1/8 teaspoon salt

Mix and serve over toast, cereal, etc.
—Note: If you use the whole flax seed, use only ⅛ cup (2 Tbs.) and grind it in a coffee grinder to give you ¼ cup of flax meal. Store in a tight container, refrigerate and use as needed.

l. _____

m. _____

11.

Nutritional Causes of Depression

- Insufficient dietary tryptophan
- Low _____n_____ intake
- _____o_____ (such depression unresponsive to medication)

n. _____

o. _____

Nature Medicine. 1997;4(7):25-30. The Lancet. 1997;349:915-919.
Journal of Clinical Psychiatry. 1998;154(4):497-501.
Am. J. Psychiatry. 1997;154:426-428. Nature. 1997;386:824-827

12.

Sources of _____p_____

Amount	Food Item	Folate (mcg)
5½ ounces	Sirloin steak, broiled, trimmed	16
½ cup	Parsnips, raw slices	44
1 cup	Pineapple juice, canned	58
1 cup	Fresh orange juice	75
¼ cup	Spanish peanuts, raw	88
1 cup	Mustard greens, raw	105
1 cup	Spinach, raw	109
1 cup	Navy beans	255
1 cup	Okra pods, frozen	269
1 cup	Lentils	831
1 cup	Black-eyed cowpeas	1057

p. _____

13.

Nutritional Causes of Depression

- Insufficient dietary tryptophan
- Low omega-3 fatty acid intake
- Low folate levels (such depression unresponsive to medication)
- Atherosclerosis causing heart disease or mini strokes

Nature Medicine. 1997;4(7):25-30. The Lancet. 1997;349:915-919.
Journal of Clinical Psychiatry. 1998;154(4):497-501.
Am. J. Psychiatry. 1997;154:426-428. Nature. 1997;386:824-827

14.

Foods Containing Harmful Cholesterol By-Products

Sources of the most harmful cholesterol to monkey aortas are:

1. _____q_____
2. _____r_____
3. _____s_____
3. __t____

q. _____

r. _____

s. _____

t. _____

15.

Foods High in _____u_____

(mg/100grams)

Lima beans	0.51
Lentils	0.54
English Walnut	0.56
Banana	0.58
Sesame seeds	0.79
Sunflower seeds	0.81
Artichoke hearts	0.94
_____v_____	2.22

0   0.5   1   1.5   2   2.5

u. _____

v. _____

16.

Nutritional Causes of Depression

- Insufficient dietary tryptophan
- Low omega-3 fatty acid intake
- Low folate levels (such depression unresponsive to medication)
- Atherosclerosis causing heart disease or mini strokes
- _____w_____ and weight loss

w. _____

Nature Medicine. 1997;4(7):25-30. The Lancet. 1997;349:915-919.
Journal of Clinical Psychiatry. 1998;154(4):497-501.
Am. J. Psychiatry. 1997;154:426-428. Nature. 1997;386:824-827

17.

Obesity Associated with Depression

- Obesity associated with low _____x_____
- After meal blood sugars in excess of 140 mg/dl associated with fatigue
- Getting on a weight loss program and losing more than _____y_____ can bring about _____z_____ levels and mood.

x. _____

y. _____

z. _____

18.

a2. _____

b2. _____

c2. _____

The Secret to Weight Loss

- Energy __a2__ must be less than energy ___b2___
- Energy expenditure must be more than energy intake
- _____c2_____ equals one pound
- 115 less calories a day equals one lb/mo

19.

d2. _____

e2. _____

f2. _____

Four Step Weight Loss Plan

- No snacks. Drink only water between meals.
- Eat a _____d2_____ and a moderate lunch. Eliminate the _____e2_____ If something "must" be eaten in the evening, whole fruit is all that is allowable.
- Eliminate or at least greatly reduce refined sugar and free fats or fatty foods in the diet, while emphasizing foods high in fiber.
- Daily moderate exercise for at least _____f2_____ a day.

20.

g2. _____

h2. _____

A Balanced Diet

One study found a substantial percentage of depressed patients' food inventories demonstrated that they consumed _____g2_____ the RDA (Recommended Daily Allowance) of one or more _____h2_____

Christensen L, Somers S. Adequacy of the dietary intake of depressed individuals. *J Am Coll Nutr* 1994 Dec;13(6):597-600

21.

Recipes

(Refer to the appendix section of
Depression: the Way Out)

22.

7. Toxic Hits

- High _____i2_____
- Battery manufacturing
- Some _____j2_____
- Dirt, dust
- Some _____k2_____

i2. _____

j2. _____

k2. _____

23.

7. Toxic Hits

- High _____l2_____
  - Some herbs, vitamins from China or India
  - Crema de Belleza Manning (Mexican facial cream)
  - Fish (bass, crappie, halibut, mackerel, pike, snapper, tuna)

l2. _____

24.

7. Toxic Hits

- High arsenic, __m2__, or other toxins

m2. _____

25.

Herbs Used for Depression

Herb	Potential Problems
Gingko Biloba Effective for mild to moderate depression	• Inhibits platelet aggregation • May cause spontaneous bleeding, reports of brain bleeding when used with aspirin • May cause minor GI side effects • Rarely, headache, dizziness, vertigo

26.

SAMe for Depression

- S-adenosyl-methionine, a naturally occurring molecule in the body made from methionine and ATP
- Short trials (one month) of 800 mg twice daily have shown _____n2_____ to standard _____o2_____
- Not advised for bipolar sufferers because of possible trigger for mania.

n2. _____

o2. _____

27.

Take Control of Your Life
- By _____ p2 _____
  - Plenty of tryptophan
  - Plenty of omega-3 foods
  - Foods high in natural carbohydrates
- By overcoming any harmful _____ q2 _____ you have
- Avoid toxins

p2. _____

q2. _____

Ↄ

What You Learned

- Foods rich in tryptophan and omega-3 are greatly beneficial to brain health, well-being and recovery from depression.
- Getting cholesterol is dangerous; but especially oxidized cholesterol. (A plant-based diet contains no cholesterol.)
- Toxic Hits can occur from sources you might not think about, such as over-the-counter medications.
- Some herbs, including gingko biloba and SAMe can benefit depression.
- By improving your diet, you can begin to take control of your life.

Ↄ

Daily Dose

Reading Prescription
- *Depression: the Way Out*: Chapter 4, Healthy Food, Better Mood: Nutritional Treatments for Depression, pages 65–77.
- Chapter of Proverbs (from the Bible) that corresponds with today's date. (Example: July 31, read Proverbs 31.) Also read a chapter of Proverbs for each day this week.
- *Telling Yourself the Truth* chapters 4 and 5.
- *SOS: Help for Emotions* chapters 7, 8, and 9.

Lifestyle Matters

Better Food, Better Mood

We've learned that food can provide the essential nutrients that our brain and body needs if we choose carefully. Concentrate this week on how you will get more tryptophan, vitamin B_{12}, omega-3, and folate in your diet and limit or eliminate the foods containing cholesterol.

1. **Tryptophan**—Page 66 of *Depression: the Way Out* shows which foods have high dietary tryptophan. Flax is also a good source of tryptophan. Which foods are you committed to eating more of starting this week? (Write more than two.)

   _____

2. **Vitamin B_{12}**—Look at the chart on page 76 of *Depression: the Way Out* and choose three good sources of vitamin B_{12} that you will begin to incorporate into your diet this week. Write your choices below.

   _____

3. **Omega-3**—The chart on page 73 of *Depression: the Way Out* shows which foods are highest in the omega-3 fatty acids. Write down the four to ten foods you will eat more of starting this week.

   _____

4. **Folic acid or folate**—Page 75 of *Depression: the Way Out* shows which foods are rich in folate. Choose four to eight of these foods you will begin consuming more of beginning today.

   _____

5. Cholesterol—Scientific research has revealed that depressed patients tend to have significantly higher bad cholesterol levels than healthy adults. Lowering bad cholesterol levels in depressed patients greatly improves treatment response in many ways.

Many of you have started making changes. Here are some steps to aid you in improving your new, healthy lifestyle.

1.   Start by eliminating meat at least two days per week.

2.   Next, start eating meat at only one meal a day.

3.   Now, eliminate meat four to five days per week.

4.   Finally, eat a total plant-based diet, and enjoy holidays with great tasting, healthy recipes.

For recipe ideas, turn to the section beginning on page 250 of *Depression: the Way Out*, and choose one or more recipes to make this week. These are great for building omega-3, serotonin, and tryptophan levels naturally and drug-free.

&

Healthy Lifestyle Scorecard   Week ___

Day	Sun	Mon	Tues	Wed	Thur	Fri	Sat
Date							
Exercise *Beginning and ending times for exercise sessions.*							
Sleep *Beginning and ending times for sleep.*							
Deep Breathing *Beginning and ending times for when you practiced deep breathing.*							
Avoided Negative Speech *Beginning and ending times for when you avoided negative speech.*							
Water *How many ounces of water you drank in a day, along with the times of day.*							
Spiritual Activity *Daily time reading Proverbs and praying. Also, write what time(s).*							
Favorite Verse							
Classical Music *Beginning and ending times for when you listened to classical music.*							
Sunlight *Beginning and ending times for sunlight or lightbox use.*							

Session Four
How Thinking Can Defeat Depression

DURING this session, pay attention to:

- If you take drug medications for depression, do they help as much as you would like?
- How using the tools of Cognitive Behavior Therapy (CBT) can dramatically change your reaction to events, as well as treat many mental health disorders.
- How you can implement these tools in your life.
- What misbeliefs you suffer with that hinder you in life.

Your *Workbook* contains the slides from Dr. Nedley's PowerPoint™ presentation for **Session Four.** Please follow along as you watch the DVD.

DVD PowerPoint™ Slides
Session Four
How Thinking Can Defeat Depression

WHILE watching Dr. Nedley's presentation, follow along with these slides that match those used in the session. If you want to, you can fill in the blanks for the missing words—sometimes a blank equals one word, other times it equals a short phrase. Use the blanks in the margins with letters that correspond to the letters on the blanks on the PowerPoint™ slides to match your answers. (For example, for blank [a] write the answer on the line to the side of the slide marked [a.], and so on.) Answers can be found in the back of this workbook.

1.

> # DEPRESSION RECOVERY
>
> How Thinking Can Defeat Depression

2.

> ### The "Easy Way"
>
> - Trap: Taking __a__ is the easy way out
> - While a medication may take away symptoms of depression, it does not cure the problem
> - Often creates a whole new array of side effects
> - Important to discover the root of the problem and treat it in a way that can bring _____b_____

a. _____

b. _____

Anti-Depressant Medication

- The _____c_____ treatment for depression
- 70 percent of patients will experience an improvement in their mood or other symptoms
- Less than 20 percent of patients on anti-depressants feel they are ___d___ or back to normal while taking the medication

3.

c._____

d._____

The Other Side of the Coin

- 25 to 30 percent _____e_____ with any ___f___
- 50 percent report bothersome side effect
  – Over one-half of these quit taking their medication
- Two-thirds not very satisfied with their treatment
- 75 percent on medication state that depression continues to impair their social life and their work performance, as well as affect family life.

4.

e._____

f._____

Relapse Rates

- Those who discontinue usage after 3 months have a 77 percent relapse rate within ___g___
- Another study showed a 40 percent relapse rate within a year.
- Even those who _____h_____ have a relapse rate of 20 to 40 percent.

5.

g._____

h._____

6.

i. _____

j. _____

k. _____

Medications Do Have Their Place

- If not used as an ___i___
- Reserved for moderate to severe depression
- Should be used in virtually all cases of ___j___
- Definite goal should be discontinuation within 6 months to a year in most cases
- If this program is carried out expect a 90 percent success rate in ___k___

7.

l. _____

m. _____

n. _____

o. _____

p. _____

The Prozac-Like Medications

Zoloft,[©] Paxil,[©] Luvox,[©] Lexapro[©] Effexor,[©] Serzone,[©] Celexa[©]

- Improves mood
- Decreases ___l___
- Decreases ___m___
- Increases ___n___
- Increases ___o___
- May cause "I don't care" attitude, ___p___ responses

American Journal of Psychiatry. 1998;155:373-379.
Clin Neuropharm. 1997;20:126-129.

8.

q. _____

r. _____

s. _____

t. _____

___q___

- Traditional forms of _____r_____ have never been shown to be ___s___ to taking a ___t___

• *Scientific American Medicine Textbook,* by Edward Rubenstein and Daniel D. Federman.

____u____ Depression

- Patients who were depressed more than two years and averaging __v__ years were studied.
- A combination of the antidepressant drug nefazodone (Serzone©) and intensive psychotherapy effectively reduces or eliminates chronic depression in _w_ % of patients.
- "We were stunned," said lead investigator Martin Keller of Brown University. "None of us had anticipated we'd show anything close to an 85% response rate for the combination."

9.

u. _____

v. _____

w. _____

Type of Psychotherapy

- Patients assigned to therapy received an intensive regimen, known as the Cognitive Behavioral Analysis System of Psychotherapy, which focuses on ____x____ .
- Not on how ____y____ shaped a person's life.
- "The focus is very much on you, and what you can ____z____ ," Keller said.
- American Psychiatric Association's annual meeting, Washington D.C. 1999

10.

x. _____

y. _____

z. _____

History of CBT

Two popular names in this history are:

- ____a2____ (Cognitive Therapy)
- ____b2____

(Rational Emotive Behavior Therapy [REBT])

11.

a2. _____

b2. _____

12.

c2. _____

d2. _____

e2. _____

Benefits of CBT

Cognitive Behavior Therapy:
- Is at least as effective as ___c2___ .
- Has no physical side-effects.
- Makes relapse less likely.
- Makes staying depression free ___d2___
- Changes ___e2___

13.

f2. _____

g2. _____

CBT Effectively Treats …

- ___f2___
- Phobias.
- Obsessive-compulsive disorder.
- Post-traumatic stress disorder.
- ___g2___
- Bulimia.

14.

h2. _____

i2. _____

j2. _____

What is Cognitive Behavior Therapy?

- A cognition is a ___h2___
- Your cognitions are the way you are thinking about things at any moment, including this ___i2___
- These thoughts have a significant impact on ___j2___

15.

Example of _____k2_____ and
_____l2_____

- "I am such a loser, I will never get better! A stupid self help depression seminar like this couldn't possibly help me. I don't have any problem with my *thoughts*, my problems are *real!*

k2. _____

l2. _____

16.

_____m2_____ and _____n2_____

- "This guy Nedley is just a con artist and he's just trying to get famous. He probably doesn't even know what he is talking about."

m2. _____

n2. _____

17.

_____o2_____ and _____p2_____

- Hey this is interesting! I might really learn something exciting and helpful!

o2. _____

p2. _____

18.

q2. _____

r2. _____

s2. _____

- Your feelings result from the ___q2___ you give yourself.
- Your thoughts have much more to do with ___r2___ , than what is actually ___s2___ in your life.

19.

What we think affects <u>who we are</u>.

20.

___t2___ ?

- You are not smart enough, successful enough, attractive enough, or talented enough to feel happy and fulfilled.
- Or your negative feelings are strictly due to others.
- Elements of truth, bad things do happen and life beats up on most of us at times.

t2. _____

21.

- All of these thoughts have the tendency to make us victims—because we think the causes result from something beyond our control.
- In contrast, you can change the way you think about things and you can also change your basic values and beliefs.
- And when you do, you will often experience lasting changes in your mood, outlook, and productivity.

22.

- Research has documented that negative thoughts which cause emotional turmoil nearly always contain ___u2___

- The thoughts on the surface appear valid, but you will learn that they are irrational or just plain wrong and that twisted thinking is a major cause of ___v2___

u2. _____

v2. _____

23.

What is it that makes your mood mad, glad, or sad?

24.

w2. _____

x2. _____

y2. _____

The A-B-C of CBT

A— ___w2___ event

A ⟶ B ⟶ C

___x2___

C—emotional ___y2___

25.

z2. _____

a3. _____

b3. _____

Cognitive Distortions

- ___z2___ thinking.
- Overgeneralization.
- ___a3___
- Disqualifying the positive.
- Jumping to conclusions. ___b3___ .

From Feeling Good, The New Mood Therapy, by David Burns, M.D.

26.

c3. _____

d3. _____

e3. _____

Cognitive Distortions

- ___c3___ error.
- Magnification or minimization.
- ___d3___ reasoning.
- Labeling and mislabeling.
- ___e3___

From Feeling Good, The New Mood Therapy, by David Burns, M.D.

27.

_____f3_____ ?

- As long as I have something to contribute to the well being of myself and others, I am not worthless.
- As long as what I do can have a positive effect, I am not worthless.
- As long as my being alive makes a difference to even one person, I am not worthless.

f3. _____

28.

Worthless?

- If I can give love, understanding, companionship, encouragement, sociability, counsel or solace, I am ___g3___ .

g3. _____

- If I can respect my opinions, I am not worthless. If others also respect, me that is a ___h3___

h3. _____

- If my presence, even just occasionally, makes a difference to others, I am not worthless.
- I am not worthless! I am eminently ___i3___

i3. _____

29.

_____j3_____

- On what facts do I base this notion?
- What are the most effective arguments I can come up with to contest this notion?
- What is the worst thing that could happen? What if it did happen? Is it likely to be as dreadful as it appears to me now?

j3. _____

30.

k3. _____

l3. _____

m3. _____

Misbelief Breakers

- What are the deeper misbeliefs that underlie my ____k3____
- Could the facts in this situation be explained in ____l3____ Are there alternative interpretations that I could give that would be more truthful and less painful. What are they?
- Have I found ____m3____ that supports or disputes this thought.

31.

n3. _____

Cognitive Distortions

- Identifying cognitive distortions is not the only task.
- The point is to *acknowledge the* ____n3____

32.

o3. _____

p3. _____

q3. _____

Truth Therapy

- ____o3____
- Get into the habit or listening to your thoughts.
- Get into the habit of noticing the ____p3____ underlying your thoughts.
- Get into the habit of challenging and replacing misbeliefs with truth.
- Get into the habit of writing all of this down.
- ____q3____

33.

Case of Someone Considering Suicide

- I would be better off dead.
- My baby would be better off without me.
- My parents don't want me and would be happier if I weren't around.
- Keith didn't want me so nobody probably ever will.
- I'll never be able to manage my life alone.

34.

- I refuse to believe I would be better off dead. My life is in God's hands. Killing myself says I know more about my baby's future than _____r3_____
- My baby wouldn't be better off without me. I am her mother and she is entitled to the best of me. We can rebuild our lives.
- Keith never knew what he wanted in a relationship and never wanted anybody for very long. I deserve better.
- I can _____s3_____

r3. _____

s3. _____

35.

Another Way to Analyze Your Thoughts...

36.

t3. _____

u3. _____

Finding the ____t3____

- What is the evidence that this thought is true or false?
- Have I had any experiences that show me that this thought is not true all the time?
- If my best friend said this, _____u3_____ to him/her?
- When I'm not feeling this way, would I think this?
- What has God said in His Word?

Adapted from, *Mind Over Mood* (1995), by D. Greenberger and C. A. Padesky.

37.

CBT is not new!

"Whatsoever things are true, whatsoever things are honest, whatsoever things are just, . . . if there be any virtue, and if there be any praise, think on these things."

Phil 4:8

38.

v3. _____

w3. _____

Steps to Using CBT

Step 3: _____v3_____

"Be transformed by the _____w3_____ "

Romans 12:2

39.

How do we renew our minds?

40.

"Whatever is ___x3___

—think about such things."

Philippians 4:8

x3. _____

41.

Finding Truth

- This is not merely ___y3___
- Find the truth, not what will make you feel better.
- Lying to yourself only delays pain and has the potential to make the reality more complicated than it needs to be.
- ___z3___ your reconstructed thought.
- The fact that you have identified a distortion means that you ___a4___ that there is a flaw in your thinking. Now ask yourself…

y3. _____

z3. _____

a4. _____

42.

What is the truth?

43.

When the Truth is ___b4___

- Sometimes this question is hard to answer.
- You may have to take time to calm yourself.

What are some methods to calm one's self quickly?

b4. _____

44.

When the Truth is Hard to Find

- Sometimes we need outside help to identify the truth.

What are some outside sources for finding truth?

45.

When the Truth is Hard to Find

- If you cannot think of any rational response to your distorted thought, write it down and then forget it for a few days.
- When you are emotionally calmer, you will be able to find the truth.
- The key is to practice reconstruction, no matter how long it takes.
- As you do it, it will become more habitual.
- As a result, your feelings will be more rational and you will have more energy and clarity to work through the stressful event.

46.

Applying CBT

Often those who have been ___c4___ for ___d4___ need to be more preventative and proactive in applying CBT to their lives.

___e4___ encountering situations where distorted thinking arises…

c4. _____

d4. _____

e4. _____

47.

Proactive CBT

What can you do?

48.

Proactive CBT

_____ f4 _____

f4. _____

49.

Proactive CBT

_____ g4 _____

g4. _____

50.

_____ h4 _____   vs.   _____ i4 _____

- The first can occur spontaneously.
- The second results from applying and reapplying the methods of accurate thinking.

h4. _____

i4. _____

51.

Steps to Using CBT

Step 4: _____j4_____

- Realistic thinking does not come naturally.
- It must be a conscious choice followed by strong effort.
- The more balanced feelings that result will be worth the struggle and the effort.

j4. _____

52.

Ancient Evidence
for the Power of Thought

"For as he thinks in his __k4__ so is he."
Proverbs 23:7, NKJV

k4. _____

ℰᴆ

What You Learned

- Cognitive Behavior Therapy (CBT) is not new. It is just as effective, if not more, than taking drug medications to solve mental health problems.
- Analyzing your thoughts to find your misbeliefs and cognitive distortions can help you restructure your thinking. Tell yourself the truth about reality, rather than lies, which only hinder you.
- Scripture is a wonderful source of truth and right thinking.
- Change takes practice, but the benefits are more than worth the struggle and effort once you see the progress you have made.

⋰

Daily Dose

Reading Prescription
- *Depression: the Way Out:* Chapter Ten, The Twenty-Week Turn Around, pages 223–233.
- *Telling Yourself the Truth* chapters 6, 7 and 8.
- Chapter of Proverbs (from the Bible) that corresponds with today's date. (Example: July 31, read Proverbs 31.) Also try to read a chapter of Proverbs for each day this week.
- *SOS: Help for Emotions* chapters 10 and 11.

Lifestyle Matters

1. A Penny for Your Thoughts

Our wrong or distorted thoughts can keep us tied to our depression and wrong behavioral patterns. The ten cognitive distortions are listed below.

- All-or-Nothing Thinking
- Overgeneralization
- Mental Filter
- Disqualifying the Positive
- Jumping to Conclusions: Mind Reading and Fortune Teller Error
- Magnification or Minimization
- Emotional Reasoning
- Should Statements
- Labeling and Mislabeling
- Personalization

Using this list and the charts below you will identify and correct thinking errors, wrong interpretations of events, and negative automatic thoughts that occur this week. Remember, the four steps of Cognitive Behavior Therapy are:

1. HEAR your internal dialogue
2. ANALYZE your internal dialogue *(and identify which cognitive distortions are present)*
3. RECONSTRUCT your thinking *(by writing down the true statements to replace the distorted thoughts)*
4. PRACTICE, practice, practice

Step 1: Think about a time where you experienced a strong negative emotion. It may have been anger, loneliness, sadness, rejection, or frustration. While recalling what you thought and felt at the time, write down your beliefs and thoughts on a separate sheet of paper (do not worry about critiquing them at this time; just record what you remember).

Step 2: Now look at this list of thoughts and beliefs you have recorded. Do you see any distortions in your thinking? If someone you knew were experiencing these in your presence right now, would you consider them rational and logical? Identify the cognitive distortions that may be involved and write them next to the erroneous belief.

Step 3: Take the distorted belief or thought and reconstruct it into a true and positive statement. Avoid using any negative terms.

(*An example*—You passed a friend on a busy street. You thought they saw you but they didn't acknowledge you when you waved hello. You concluded that they were mad at you. Probably this is not true but it hurt your feelings just the same. The belief might be: "Sally didn't return my greeting and is mad at me or doesn't like me anymore. I feel worthless and unlovable." The distortion involved could be "Mind Reading" which is a "Jumping to Conclusions" error. A possible reconstruction could be: "Sally might have had something else on her mind and didn't even notice my wave. But even if she had seen me and ignored me, I am still a worthwhile person who has positive qualities to bring to a friendship.")

ↄ

2. Accentuate the Positive, Eliminate the Negative

Our thoughts and our behaviors are related. ("For as the thoughts of his heart are, so is he." —Proverbs 23:7) You may have learned many new things in this session. Practicing these CBT exercises should help you manage your negative thoughts. This in turn will help you not speak harsh, critical words about anything or anyone.

a. Have you successfully gone two weeks without speaking any critical, negative comments? We started this exercise in Session One.

yes   no

b. If you have, congratulations. You have no doubt noticed what a change has come to your mind. Maintaining this healthy new habit can really benefit those who are depressed. Make sure to pay close attention to the *constructive criticism* you now use so that it does not slip into *destructive criticism.*

c. If your answer was *no,* don't give up. You are probably much more aware now when you get ready to utter those negative statements than you were before. Each day you attempt this exercise, your mind is being trained into a new pattern of thought. (Review the instructions from the Lifestyle Matters section on page 29 to reacquaint yourself with the keys to success.) When you catch yourself saying something critical and have to start over your 14 day count, start that hour. Don't be tempted to let the rest of the day go by being as critical as you used to be.

• What is a cognition? _____

_____

• What makes your mood glad, mad, or sad? _____

_____

_____

The ABCs of CBT (Activating event, Beliefs, Consequences.)

• List an event that made you glad, mad or sad. _____

_____

_____

• What was your belief about that event? _____

_____

- What were the consequences of the situation? _____

_____

_____

_____

_____

- Did the consequences make you mad, glad or sad? On what facts did you base this notion? Remember to think about what has offended you. Ask yourself, "How would I have taken this if my best friend has said or done this to me?"

- Remember these tips that will help you calm down: deep breathing (at least three deep breaths) and brisk walking.

- Cognitive Behavior Therapy (CBT) makes staying depression-free more likely. Practice the ABCs of CBT. The more you practice, the easier it gets to eliminate distorted thinking.

Tips for Success: This is the halfway point for our eight week program. Full recovery can take up to 20 weeks and each person's depression is as individual as he or she is. The most important thing is to *never give up.*

Healthy Lifestyle Scorecard   **Week** ___

Day	Sun	Mon	Tues	Wed	Thur	Fri	Sat
Date							
Exercise *Beginning and ending times for exercise sessions.*							
Sleep *Beginning and ending times for sleep.*							
Deep Breathing *Beginning and ending times for when you practiced deep breathing.*							
Avoided Negative Speech *Beginning and ending times for when you avoided negative speech.*							
Water *How many ounces of water you drank in a day, along with the times of day.*							
Spiritual Activity *Daily time reading Proverbs and praying. Also, write what time(s).*							
Favorite Verse							
Classical Music *Beginning and ending times for when you listened to classical music.*							
Sunlight *Beginning and ending times for sunlight or lightbox use.*							

Session Five
Positive Lifestyle Choices

DURING this session, pay attention to:

- The stages of change—can you recognize these in your life?
- Whether you engage in moderation and when this is even possible.
- What pleasures you choose—temporary or eternal?
- Whether you might have any addictions.

Your *Workbook* contains the slides from Dr. Nedley's PowerPoint™ presentation for **Session Five.** Please follow along as you watch the DVD.

DVD PowerPoint™ Slides
Session Five
Positive Lifestyle Choices

WHILE watching Dr. Nedley's presentation, follow along with these slides that match those used in the session. If you want to, you can fill in the blanks for the missing words—sometimes a blank equals one word, other times it equals a short phrase. Use the blanks in the margins with letters that correspond to the letters on the blanks on the PowerPoint™ slides to match your answers. (For example, for blank [a] write the answer on the line to the side of the slide marked [a.], and so on.) Answers can be found in the back of this workbook.

1.

DEPRESSION RECOVERY

Positive Lifestyle Choices

2.

Major Depression--constellation of symptoms

The Ten "Hit" Categories

1. Genetic
2. Developmental
3. Lifestyle
4. Circadian rhythm
5. Addiction
6. Nutrition
7. Toxic
8. Social/Complicated Grief
9. Medical Condition
10. Frontal Lobe

3.

The Struggle

- Learning ___a___ .
- Getting ___b___ .
- ___c___

4.

a. _____

b. _____

c. _____

CHANGE

5.

6.

d. _____

e. _____

f. _____

g. _____

Stages of Change

- Precontemplation
- _____d_____
- _____e_____
- _____f_____
- _____g_____

7.

h. _____

i. _____

j. _____

k. _____

5. Addiction Hits

- Alcohol
- _____h_____
- _____i_____
- _____j_____
- _____k_____

8.

l. _____

m. _____

n. _____

_____l_____ that may require medical help

- _____m_____
- _____n_____
- Benzodiazepines (Xanax[©] Valium[©] Ativan[©] Klonopin[©] Paxipam[©] Librium[©])

Overcoming Addictions Requires Understanding of Temperance

- ___o___ in the use of ___P___ substances
- ___q___ (complete) from ___r___ substances

9.

o. _____

p. _____

q. _____

r. _____

Why Abstinence from the unhealthy?

- First, because it is ___s___
- Second, because of the ___t___ nature of ___u___

10.

s. _____

t. _____

u. _____

Common Characteristics of Addictions

1. Overwhelming compulsion to ___v___
2. Need for ___w___
3. ___x___ (withdrawal)
4. High tendency to ___y___
5. Detrimental effect on individual/society

11.

v. _____

w. _____

x. _____

y. _____

12.

z. _____

a2. _____

b2. _____

c2. _____

The Call for Moderation

- A person who has a _____z_____ relationship can no more use it "moderately" than an ___a2___ can return to moderate drinking or a _____b2_____ can return to moderate smoking.
- In dealing with any addictive habit, total _____c2_____ is necessary.

13.

d2. _____

e2. _____

Choosing our own pleasures

- We have the ability to choose our own pleasures
- If we reward ourselves with a ___d2___ periodically, we undermine our ability to develop ___e2___ for a lifestyle that is free of that agent.

14.

f2. _____

g2. _____

h2. _____

What about just once a month?

- Certainly an improvement
- But the desire is being _____f2_____
- And may even be increased giving rise to feelings of a deep distressing sense of deprivation
- If the addiction is _____g2_____ and the thoughts directed toward the joy of being free, the addiction will soon _____h2_____

15.

Recommend Giving Up
All Addictions at the Same Time
• Lifestyle Center of America Study of Caffeine and Tobacco

16.

Ten Ways to Kick the ___i2___
Out of Kicking the Habit

1. ____j2____
2. No hidden cigarettes
3. Deep breathing
4. Daily exercise (walking)
5. Get more sleep
6. Water inside
7. Water outside
8. Avoid:
   – ___k2___
   – alcohol
   – heavy meal
   – heavily spiced foods

9. Avoid ___l2___ situations such as:
   – special chairs
   – work breaks
   – people who smoke
10. Expect that others will understand

i2._____

j2._____

k2._____

l2._____

17.

But What If?

18.

m2. _____

n2. _____

o2. _____

Overcoming Addiction

- Need to have knowledge that the habit is ___m2___
- Need to choose to overcome
- Need to rely on _____n2_____
- Let go, and ___o2___

19.

p2. _____

q2. _____

Victory Over Battles

"But thanks be to God, which giveth us the ___p2___ through our Lord ___q2___"

1 Corinthians 15:57

20.

r2. _____

s2. _____

t2. _____

u2. _____

___r2___ for the ___s2___

"If ye then, being evil, know how to give good gifts unto your children, how much ___t2___ shall your Father which is in heaven give good things to them that ___u2___ him?"

Matthew 7:11

___v2___ Makes no Provision to _w2_

"But put ye on the Lord Jesus Christ, and make not provision for the flesh, to fulfil the lusts thereof."

Romans 13:14

21.

v2. _____

w2. _____

I Peter 4:1-2

"Forasmuch then as Christ hath suffered for us in the flesh, arm yourselves likewise
_____x2_____:
For he that hath suffered in the flesh
hath ceased from sin;
that he no longer should live the rest of his time ___y2___
to the lusts
of men,
but to ___z2_____ "

22.

x2. _____

y2. _____

z2. _____

Turning Defeat into Victory

"If you have made mistakes,
you certainly gain a
___a3___
if you see these mistakes and regard them
as beacons of ___b3___
Thus you turn defeat into victory, disappointing the enemy and honoring your
___c3___ "

E.G. White, Christ's Object Lessons p. 332

23.

a3. _____

b3. _____

c3. _____

24.

d3. _____

e3. _____

f3. _____

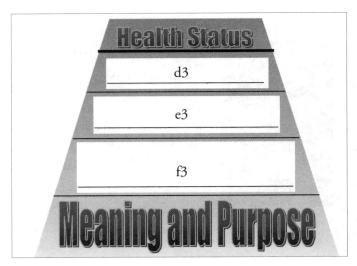

❧

What You Learned

- Change is a struggle that requires commitment.
- Overcoming addictions requires understanding temperance.
- Alcohol, tobacco, caffeine, and even some medications can be habit forming and cause addiction.
- Faith and strength are a gift from God and can turn defeat into victory.

❧

Daily Dose

Reading Prescription
- *Depression: the Way Out*: Chapter 7, Stress and Anxiety, pages 125–144.
- Chapter of Proverbs (from the Bible) that corresponds with today's date. (Example: July 31, read Proverbs 31.) Also try to read a chapter of Proverbs for each day this week.
- *Telling Yourself the Truth* chapters 9 and 10.
- *SOS: Help for Emotions–Managing Anxiety, Anger & Depression* by Lynn Clark, Ph.D. By now you should be finished reading this book, but if you have not, try to finish this week.

Lifestyle Matters

1. ***Another way*** **of looking at the Stages of Change (first referred to on slide 6) is outlined below:**

   Stage 1: Unconsciously Incompetent (Pre-contemplation)
   Stage 2: Consciously Incompetent (Contemplation)
   Stage 3: Consciously Competent (Preparation)
   Stage 4: Unconsciously Competent (Action)

   To move from Unconsciously Incompetent (**Stage 1**) to being Consciously Incompetent (**Stage 2**) you must be informed. The Bible says, "My people are destroyed for lack of knowledge."

   Take the power of positive thinking as an example. Suppose someone tells you that you often focus on the negative. If in the past you had frequently made negative statements, you were in **Stage 1**—you had not yet realized that you were focusing on the negative. Now, if it is brought to your attention and you realize what you have been doing, you move to Consciously Incompetent (**Stage 2**) because you are aware of your actions, although you have not implemented a change at this point.

   To move from **Stage 2** to Consciously Competent (**Stage 3**), you must rely upon God for strength, and do what you can to change. It is often difficult, and during this time you are conscious of the fact that you are changing. You will catch yourself and consciously take the time to make positive statements—you think about it before responding.

   Once your change becomes habit, eventually you will no longer be tempted to go back to **Stage 2**. That is when you move to Unconsciously Competent (**Stage 4**). It is part of your life—it is easy—and you are experiencing the benefits of the change.

   > Read "Four Ways to
   > Improve Social Wellness"
   > from page xiv.

2. Kicking the Habit

a. Each of us can recognize the harmful practices that we do. When these harmful practices are repeated on a regular basis, they are often classifiable as addictions.

b. Take a moment and list any addictions you would like to overcome:

_____

_____

c. How strong is your desire to eliminate these addictions? Using a scale of 0 to 10 with 0 being "none" and 10 being "very strong" mark each addiction above and circle your number rating.

d. Take the addiction with the highest score and use next exercise to start a plan.

The Plan:

1. Starting today, choose an addiction that you would like to eliminate.

   (The day/date I will stop _____

   _____ (addiction)

   is _____ .)

2. Refer to the keys to quitting (see slide number 16, Ten Ways to Kick the Misery Out of Kicking the Habit) and review them on a daily basis. Practice them faithfully.

A verse to encourage you:
"I can do all things through Christ who strengthens me."
—*Philippians 4:13*

3. Review from Previous Sessions

In the previous weeks, you have taken into account Lifestyle Matters, all relating to depression recovery. The Lifestyle Matters are listed below. Please circle the answer for each item to indicate whether you have or have not been taking part in these activities. (The superscript number indicates the session where each Lifestyle Matter is found.)

a.	No critical or negative speech[1]	*Doing*	*Not Doing*
b.	Classical music therapy[1]	*Doing*	*Not Doing*
c.	Adequate water intake[1]	*Doing*	*Not Doing*
d.	Exercise and intermittent training (I.T.)[1,2]	*Doing*	*Not Doing*
e.	Deep breathing exercises[2]	*Doing*	*Not Doing*
f.	Light therapy; good light exposure[2]	*Doing*	*Not Doing*
g.	Massage[2]	*Doing*	*Not Doing*
h.	Contrast Showers[2]	*Doing*	*Not Doing*
i.	Tryptophan intake[3]	*Doing*	*Not Doing*
j.	Vitamin B_{12} intake[3]	*Doing*	*Not Doing*
k.	Omega-3 intake[3]	*Doing*	*Not Doing*
l.	Folic acid intake[3]	*Doing*	*Not Doing*
m.	Cholesterol intake reduced/eliminated[3]	*Doing*	*Not Doing*
n.	Plant-based diet[3]	*Doing*	*Not Doing*

- **On page 118, write out a plan for each Lifestyle Matter you need to adopt. Write a day/date that you will incorporate your new lifestyle habits.**
- **Review the suggestions made in the corresponding sections of the workbook and *Depression: the Way Out*.**

Healthy Lifestyle Scorecard   Week ___

Day	Sun	Mon	Tues	Wed	Thur	Fri	Sat
Date							
Exercise *Beginning and ending times for exercise sessions.*							
Sleep *Beginning and ending times for sleep.*							
Deep Breathing *Beginning and ending times for when you practiced deep breathing.*							
Avoided Negative Speech *Beginning and ending times for when you avoided negative speech.*							
Water *How many ounces of water you drank in a day, along with the times of day.*							
Spiritual Activity *Daily time reading Proverbs and praying. Also, write what time(s).*							
Favorite Verse							
Classical Music *Beginning and ending times for when you listened to classical music.*							
Sunlight *Beginning and ending times for sunlight or lightbox use.*							

Session Six
Stress without Distress

DURING this session, pay attention to:

- Your sleep habits and how they might affect melatonin production.
- Whether your diet supplies enough calcium.
- Situations in your life where you can employ the stress-reduction techniques outlined in this session.
- When you might spend time on trivial events when there are more important tasks to accomplish.

Your *Workbook* contains the slides from Dr. Nedley's PowerPoint™ presentation for **Session Six.** Please follow along as you watch the DVD.

DVD PowerPoint™ Slides
Session Six
Stress without Distress

WHILE watching Dr. Nedley's presentation, follow along with these slides that match those used in the session. If you want to, you can fill in the blanks for the missing words—sometimes a blank equals one word, other times it equals a short phrase. Use the blanks in the margins with letters that correspond to the letters on the blanks on the PowerPoint™ slides to match your answers. (For example, for blank [a] write the answer on the line to the side of the slide marked [a.], and so on.) Answers can be found in the back of this workbook.

1.

DEPRESSION RECOVERY

Stress without Distress

2.

Coping with Stress Naturally

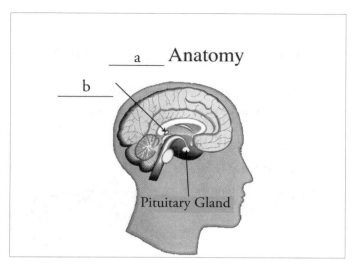

3.

a. _____

b. _____

Pineal Gland Secretions

- Epithalamin
  - Protein thought to increase learning capacity and slow down aging
- ___c___
  - Elevates mood and has influence on sleep and pain
- Arginine Vasotocin
  - Potent protein capable of rapidly inducing deep sleep
- ___d___
  - The "fix and rejuvenate" night-time hormone

4.

c. _____

d. _____

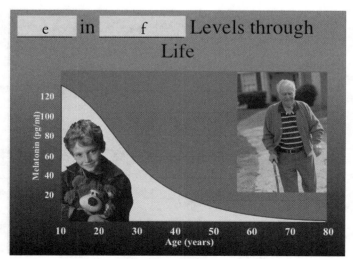

___e___ in ___f___ Levels through Life

5.

e. _____

f. _____

6.

g._____

h._____

i._____

Probable Effects of Melatonin

- Protects against free radical damage from certain carcinogens, herbicides, and ___g___
- Prevents or helps fight ___h___
- Delays some effects of aging
- ___i___ enhancer

7.

j._____

k._____

l._____

Probable Effects of Melatonin

- Assists in coping with ___j___
- Increases the ability to experience ___k___
- Lowers cholesterol, blood pressure, and risk of heart rhythm problems
- Lowers risk of ___l___

8.

Melatonin Level Variations Throughout the Day

Melatonin (pg/ml)

80 70 60 50 40 30 20 10 0

2:00 PM · Darkness · 2:00 AM · 7:00 AM

Time of Day

Sleep is Better Before Midnight

"Sleep is worth far more before than after midnight. _____m_____ good sleep before twelve o'clock is worth more than _____n_____ after twelve o'clock…"

Ellen G White 7MR 224

9.

m. _____

n. _____

Steps in the Production of Melatonin

1. The pineal gland draws _____o_____ an amino acid, from the blood.

2. Tryptophan is converted to _____p_____ in the gland. This reaction is light-dependant.

3. Serotonin is converted to _____q_____

4. Step 3 requires darkness, sufficient calcium, and Vitamin B-6

10.

o. _____

p. _____

q. _____

Calcium in Common Foods

Food Item	Amount	Mg
Oatmeal	1c.	19
Lentils	1c.	38
Quinoa grain	1c.	102
Rutabagas	1c.	115
Dandelion greens	1c.	147
Mustard greens	1c.	152
Baked beans	1c.	154
Sesame seeds (dried)	2Tbs.	176
Blackstrap cane molasses	1Tbs.	176
Kale	1c.	179

11.

12.

Calcium in Common Foods

Food Item	Amount	Mg
Turnip greens	1c.	249
Filberts/Hazelnuts (dried)	1c.	254
Green soybeans	1c.	261
Figs (dried)	10	269
Whole milk	1c.	290
Amaranth grain	1c.	298
Nonfat skim milk	1c.	301
Collard greens	1c.	357
Carob flour	1c.	358
Lambsquarters	1c.	464

13.

r. _____

s. _____

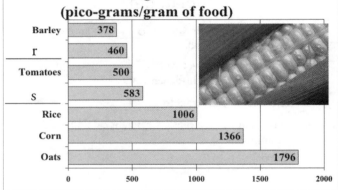

Foods High in Melatonin
(pico-grams/gram of food)

Food	pico-grams/gram
Barley	378
r	460
Tomatoes	500
s	583
Rice	1006
Corn	1366
Oats	1796

14.

Lifestyle Factors that Reduce the Melatonin Peak

- _____t_____
- _____u_____
  - Cuts melatonin production in half for 6 hours
- _____v_____
  - Up to 41 percent reduction
- _____w_____

15.

t. _____

u. _____

v. _____

w. _____

Certain types of ___x___ may actually be ___y___ for you

- People experience passive stress when watching a scary movie, while active stress is what an individual feels when they are busy trying to meet a deadline.
- 30 male volunteers aged 18 to 34 who were exposed to two different types of stressful situations. In the active stressful event, volunteers were asked to memorize information and take a 12-minute test.
- For the passive stressful event, they watched a 12-minute video of "gruesome" surgical procedures.

16.

x. _____

y. _____

- During the experiments, each person gave saliva samples that where analyzed for immune system components known as _____z_____ These proteins help protect the lining of organs such as the lungs and stomach, guarding against the invasion of bacteria and viruses while possibly fighting ___a2___
- While levels of secretory proteins increased during active stress, the _____b2_____ actually dropped during passive stress.

17.

z. _____

a2. _____

b2. _____

127

18.

- "Stress is not the _____c2_____ everybody is thinking it is--in fact, most acute stressors boost the immune system."
- "Only when the stress is _____d2_____ or repetitive it becomes a potential threat to health."
- One exception is the body's reaction to acute stressors to which there is no way of responding, except to passively endure. These types of stressors, which people might describe by using the phrase "my heart stopped beating," have a rapid and strong suppressive effect on some aspects of immune function.

c2. _____

d2. _____

19.

Quotes from the author

- "Instead of advising ways of ___e2___ stress I would like people to consider ways of ___f2___ stress."
- "Such events boost the immune system and may be good to your health."
- Dr. Jos A. Bosch of Ohio State University

Psychophysiology 2001;38:836-846

e2. _____

f2. _____

20.

Stress Control

- _____g2_____ that can be ___h2___ improves the immune system
- Piling on of active stressors so that sleep, exercise, or the devotional life suffers will eventually impair the ___i2___

g2. _____

h2. _____

i2. _____

21.

Drugs and Supplements that Reduce Melatonin

- Non-steroidal anti-inflammatory drugs
- Beta & Calcium Channel Blockers
- Anti-anxiety drugs & ___j2___
- ___k2___ (3 mg a day)
- ___l2___

j2. _____

k2. _____

l2. _____

22.

Habits that Increase Melatonin Production

- Increase exposure to ___m2___ and minimize exposure to ___n2___
- Sleep in complete darkness.
- Eat foods rich in melatonin, tryptophan, and ___o2___
- Avoid a calcium deficiency.
- Restrict food intake in general.
- Practice fasting, especially in evening hours.

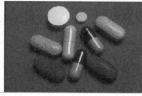

m2. _____

n2. _____

o2. _____

23.

Neil Nedley, M.D.

PROOF POSITIVE:

How to Reliably Combat Disease and Achieve Optimal Health through Nutrition and Lifestyle

Call Toll-free
1-888-778-4445

EDITED BY DAVID DeROSE, M.D.
Digital imagery® ©1999 PhotoDisc, Inc.

24.

p2. _____

q2. _____

r2. _____

Reactions to Stressors

Phase 1 · ___p2___

Phase 2 · ___q2___

Phase 3 · ___r2___

25.

s2. _____

t2. _____

u2. _____

___s2___ Can Contribute to these
___t2___ · ___u2___

- Cardiovascular diseases
- Cancer
- Depression
- Diabetes mellitus
- Hip fracture
- Tuberculosis
- Rheumatoid arthritis
- AIDS

26.

v2. _____

w2. _____

x2. _____

Stress can contribute to or aggravate these Ailments

- Muscle related conditions
- ___v2___
- Irritable Bowel Syndrome
- Premenstrual tension syndrome
- ___w2___   Health
- Warts
- ___x2___
- Psoriasis
- Gout
- Herpes

27.

Stress Control Measures

1. Healthy adaptation

28.

Stress Control Techniques

- _____y2_____ the Stressor
  - Landlord
  - Confront Directly
  - Move
- Healthy Adaptation
  - Change bedtime to 9 p.m.
- ___z2___ the Stressor rarely the best
  response

y2. _____

z2. _____

29.

Stress Control Measures

1. Healthy adaptation
2. Healthy ___a3___

a3. _____

30.

Will Involve

- Learning More About the Brain
- Making Choices
- Building Relationships

31.

b3. _____

c3. _____

d3. _____

e3. _____

f3. _____

g3. _____

___b3___ for ___c3___

- ___d3___ is suggested for loss of ___e3___ nervousness, and insomnia. 3 to 5 gms a day.
- ___f3___ is recommended for nervousness and insomnia. 8 to 10 gms a day.
- ___g3___ can help nervousness, insomnia, stress, and anxiety. 600 mg to 15 gms a day.

32.

h3. _____

i3. _____

j3. _____

___h3___ for Stress or Anxiety

- Avoid Benzodiazepines (Xanax©, Valium©, Ativan©, Klonopin©, Paxipam©, Librium©)
- SSRIs such as Paxil© or ___i3___
- **Remeron© (if insomnia and anorexia)**
- TCAs
- ___j3___
-

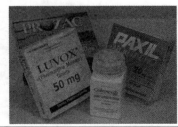

Isaiah 58

10   And if thou draw out thy soul to the hungry, and satisfy the afflicted soul; then shall thy light rise in obscurity, and thy darkness be as the noonday:

11   And the LORD shall guide thee ___k3___ , and satisfy thy soul in drought, and make fat thy ___l3___ and thou shalt be like a watered garden, and like a spring of water, whose waters fail not.

33.

k3. _____

l3. _____

Stress Control

1. Healthy adaptation

2. Healthy lifestyle, including good nutrition and exercise

3. Commitment to an ___m3___ that helps others and is morally sound.

34.

m3. _____

Proper ___n3___ and Organization

"For which of you, intending to build a tower, sitteth not down first, and counteth the cost, whether he have sufficient to finish it?"

Luke 14:28

35.

n3. _____

36.

Stress Control

1. Healthy adaptation

2. Healthy lifestyle, including good nutrition and exercise

3. Commitment to an honorable cause that helps others and is morally sound.

4. Proper planning and organization

37.

o3. _____

"Take therefore no thought o3 : for the morrow shall take thought for the things of itself."

Matthew 6:34

38.

Stress Control

1. Healthy adaptation

2. Healthy lifestyle, including good nutrition and exercise

3. Commitment to an honorable cause that helps others and is morally sound.

4. Proper planning and organization

5. Don't be anxious about tomorrow

Dwell on the ___p3___

"Finally brethren, whatsoever things are true, whatsoever things are honest, whatsoever things are just, whatsoever things are pure, whatsoever things are lovely, whatsoever things are of good report; if there be any virtue, and if there be any praise, think on these things."

Phil 4:8

39.

p3._____

Stress Control

1. Healthy adaptation
2. Healthy lifestyle, including good nutrition and exercise
3. Commitment to an honorable cause that helps others and is morally sound.
4. Proper planning and organization
5. Don't be anxious about tomorrow
6. Dwell on the good

40.

7. Meditation
___q3___

41.

q3_____

42.

When to be Anxious

"Be anxious for ___r3___, but in everything by prayer and supplication with thanksgiving let your requests be made known to God."
Philippians 4:6

r3. _____

43.

Examples in Stress Control

24   **Five times received I forty stripes save one.**

25   **Thrice was I beaten with rods, once was I stoned, thrice I suffered shipwreck, a night and a day I have been in the deep;**

26   **In journeyings often, in perils of waters, in perils of robbers, in perils by mine own countrymen, in perils by the heathen, in perils in the city, in perils in the wilderness, in perils in the sea, in perils among false brethren;**

27   **In weariness and painfulness, in watchings often, in hunger and thirst, in fastings often, in cold and nakedness.**

2 Cor 11

44.

8. Trust in God

"We are troubled on every side,
yet ___s3___ ;
we are perplexed,
but ___t3___ ;
Persecuted, ___u3___ ;
cast down, but not destroyed."
2 Corinthians 4:8,9

s3. _____

t3. _____

u3. _____

45.

Romans 8:37

Nay, in all these things we are ___v3___ _____ through him that loved us.

v3. _____

46.

Come Unto Me

"Come unto me, all ye that labour and are ___w3___ , and I will give you ___x3___
Matthew 11:28

w3. _____

x3. _____

47.

This is no time for the ___y3___

- After the WTC attack TV talk show hosts were saying, "What I do is so trivial".
- Talk show guests (movie stars) were refusing to appear because what they do is "so trivial."
- The Sports World admitted that the games they play are "so trivial".
- If they admit it, why do we continue to waste our time with the trivial?
- It is time for the important things in life!

y3. _____

48.

z3. _____

Stress Control

- Healthy adaptation
- Healthy lifestyle, including good nutrition and exercise
- Commitment to an honorable cause that helps others and is morally sound
- Proper planning and organization
- Don't worry about results
- Dwell on the good
- Meditation and Prayer
- ___z3___

❧

What You Learned

- Some stress can be either positive or negative, depending on how we respond to it.
- Prolonged, unhealthy stress can lead to a myriad of diseases.
- The impact of stress can be lessened through a healthy lifestyle including good nutrition, exercise, liberal use of water, daily exposure to sunlight, temperance, deep breathing (and fresh air), adequate rest, and trust in God.
- Adaptations and expectations can change the way stress affects us.
- There are many useful tools for relieving stress.

❧

Daily Dose

Reading Prescription

- *Depression: the Way Out*: Chapter Eight: Stress without Distress, pages 147–171.

- *Telling Yourself the Truth* chapters 11 and 12.

- Chapter of Proverbs (from the Bible) that corresponds with today's date. (Example: July 31, read Proverbs 31.) Also try to read a chapter of Proverbs for each day this week.

Lifestyle Matters

We've already seen that tryptophan is important in overcoming depression and optimizing brain function because of its role in brain chemistry. Without sufficient dietary tryptophan, our bodies don't make enough serotonin. Serotonin is a **neurotransmitter**—a brain chemical that carries messages between brain cells. This important chemical regulates mood, appetite, aggression, body temperature, and sleep. Low levels of serotonin in the brain are associated with feelings of depression.

The human body converts serotonin into melatonin, another important brain and body chemical. Melatonin, a hormone, is involved in the sleep/wakefulness cycle (also known as the *circadian rhythm*) and acts as an antioxidant. Decreased levels of melatonin during the night can cause difficulty falling asleep and reduce the restfulness of sleep. There is scientific evidence that melatonin boosts immune system function, lowers cholesterol in people with high levels and may be useful in treating or preventing cancer.

In order for serotonin to be converted into melatonin conditions must be right. We need to have enough dietary calcium, vitamin B_6, and proper darkness at sleep time. This week you need to concentrate on the healthy habits that make this possible.

1. Calcium

> Read "Four Ways to Improve Physical Wellness" from page xv.

In your *Depression: the Way Out* on page 170 you'll find the foods that are highest in calcium. Read the chart and decide which 5 to 10 foods you will consume more of starting this week. List these foods here:

_____

_____

_____

2. Melatonin

We can get more melatonin in our foods as well. Refer to the chart on slide number 13 in this session's presentation for the foods highest in melatonin.

Barley, bananas, tomatoes, ginger root, brown rice, corn, and oats are all good sources of melatonin. Are you getting plenty of these foods in your diet? If you're not, incorporate these into your diet starting today.

3. Sleep

Sleep is important in managing stress, regulating body and brain function, and enabling the body to make melatonin out of serotonin. We need to follow the rules of good quality sleep. They are:

a. Sleep in a very dark, cool, tidy, comfortable, and quiet environment.

b. Provide fresh air in your sleeping room.

c. Increase exposure to natural light during daylight hours (or get bright light therapy if not able to enjoy natural outdoor light.)

d. Every hour of sleep before 12 midnight is worth two hours after midnight, so get to bed earlier.

e. Set anxieties and worries aside as you get in bed and make sure your conscience is clear.

f. Eliminate the three chief sleep robbers: alcohol, tobacco, and caffeine.

g. Restrict food intake during the evening meal and don't eat for several hours before bed.

h. Maintain a regular schedule for bedtime and waking time.

i. Insure vigorous, daily physical exercise.

j. Make sure that none of the medications you take interfere with sleep.

Are you currently violating any of these ten commandments for good quality sleep?   yes   no

Circle the letters of the ones you find challenging.

Choose some to correct this week.

_____

_____

_____

_____

☙

Healthy Lifestyle Scorecard   Week ___

Day	Sun	Mon	Tues	Wed	Thur	Fri	Sat
Date							
Exercise *Beginning and ending times for exercise sessions.*							
Sleep *Beginning and ending times for sleep.*							
Deep Breathing *Beginning and ending times for when you practiced deep breathing.*							
Avoided Negative Speech *Beginning and ending times for when you avoided negative speech.*							
Water *How many ounces of water you drank in a day, along with the times of day.*							
Spiritual Activity *Daily time reading Proverbs and praying. Also, write what time(s).*							
Favorite Verse							
Classical Music *Beginning and ending times for when you listened to classical music.*							
Sunlight *Beginning and ending times for sunlight or lightbox use.*							

143

Session Seven
Living Above Loss

DURING this session, pay attention to:

- The losses you've experienced in your life, and how you've reacted.
- Whether you have any cognitive distortions that affect your abilities.
- If you have made use of all of the different tasks of mourning.
- How you can grow from your losses.

Your *Workbook* contains the slides from Dr. Nedley's PowerPoint™ presentation for **Session Seven.** Please follow along as you watch the DVD.

DVD PowerPoint™ Slides
Session Seven
Living Above Loss

WHILE watching Dr. Nedley's presentation, follow along with these slides that match those used in the session. If you want to, you can fill in the blanks for the missing words—sometimes a blank equals one word, other times it equals a short phrase. Use the blanks in the margins with letters that correspond to the letters on the blanks on the PowerPoint™ slides to match your answers. (For example, for blank [a] write the answer on the line to the side of the slide marked [a.], and so on.) Answers can be found in the back of this workbook.

1.

> # DEPRESSION RECOVERY
>
> Living Above Loss

2.

> ## The Ten "Hit" Categories
>
> 1. Genetic
> 2. Developmental
> 3. Lifestyle
> 4. Circadian rhythm
> 5. Addiction
> 6. Nutrition
> 7. Toxic
> 8. Social/Complicated Grief
> 9. Medical Condition
> 10. Frontal Lobe

8. Social Hits Increase the Risk of Depression

- Absence of _____a_____
- Negative, stressful life events
- Grandparents who raise their grandchildren
- Immediate family member that you live with is an _____b_____
- Suffered critical loss, such as a loved one or treasured job within the last 18 months

British Medical Journal. 1998;316:1-5. Journal of the American Academy of Child and Adolescent Psychiatry. 1998;37:473-487.
J Am Acad Child Adolesc Psychiatry. 1997;36:255-262. J Am Acad Child Adolesc Psychiatry. 1996;35(12):1602-1610.
Archives of General Psychiatry. 1998;55:161-166. Arch General Psychiatry. 1997;54:124-130.
Molecular Psychiatry. 1998;3:86-91. Archives of Family Medicine. 1997;6:445-452.

3.

a. _____

b. _____

How to Overcome Loss

4.

Definitions

___c___ an emotional reaction that follows the loss of someone or something of great value.

_____d_____ the psychological process that occurs when you experience loss.

5.

c. _____

d. _____

6.

e. _____

f. _____

g. _____

Types of Losses

- Loss of social status.
- Loss of __e__
- Loss of the ability to maintain a physical function.
- Loss of __f__
- Loss of a home.
- Loss of a __g__

7.

h. _____

i. _____

Cognitive Distortions

- Some beliefs are ____h____ and *will* lead to _____i_____ -- for instance...

8.

j. _____

k. _____

_____j_____ vs. ____k____

"I'm losing an important part of my life."

"My world has ended."
"I can't live without her."

9.

- "I will miss the companionship and love that we shared."—tender, realistic, desirable, will ___l___ your humanity and add depth to the meaning of life.
- "I will never again be happy because she (or he) died. It's unfair."—Trigger thoughts of self pity and hopelessness. These thoughts are based on distortions and will __m__ you.

l. _____

m. _____

10.

11.

The ________ is required for __o__ .

n. _____

o. _____

12.

13.

p. _____

q. _____

_____p_____ Vs. _____q_____

14.

r. _____

s. _____

t. _____

Stages of Grief

Stage 1—Shock & Disbelief:

- Events seem unreal.
- Feeling _____r_____
- _____s_____
- Crying.
- Anger.
- _____t_____

15.

Stages of Grief

Stage 2—Developing Awareness:

- Duration of ___u___ months.
- Preoccupation with the loss.
- Anxiety.
- Restlessness.
- Difficulty ___v___ .

u. _____

v. _____

16.

Stages of Grief

Possible Characteristics of Stage 2:

- Loss of appetite.
- ___w___
- ___x___
- ___y___
- ___z___

w. _____

x. _____

y. _____

z. _____

17.

Stages of Grief

Possible Characteristics of Stage 2:

- Identification with the lost loved one.
- A ___a2___ response on the anniversary of the loss.
- A ___b2___ awareness of the loss.
- Recognition of the ___c2___ of the loss.
- Mood swings.

a2. _____

b2. _____

c2. _____

18.

d2. _____

Stages of Grief

**The Good News about
Stage 2**
Although long in duration,
you should gradually feel
better _____ d2 _____.

19.

e2. _____

f2. _____

g2. _____

Stages of Grief

Stage 3—Resolution:
- From 3 to 12 months after the loss.
- Incorporation of _____ e2 _____
- _____ f2 _____ changes.
- Making _____ g2 _____

20.

h2. _____

i2. _____

j2. _____

Stages of Grief

The _____ h2 _____ about Stage 3

You gradually take ___ i2 ___ of your life and
resolve the loss, through ___ j2 ___ ,
readjustment, and education.

Lessons of Grief

- 40 men whose immune systems were already compromised were studied from 4 to 9 years after they had experienced tragic loss.
- Grief over the loss of a loved one is often followed by _____k2_____ , and a _____l2_____ of life's worth and meaning.

21.

k2. _____

l2. _____

Lessons of Grief

- 65% of the men had engaged in a thoughtful consideration of the meaning of their loved one's death
- A process the authors call " _____m2_____ "
- This type of reflection can lead individuals to _____n2_____ .

22.

m2. _____

n2. _____

Lessons of Grief

Group 1: For some their loved one's death only emphasized the _____o2_____

Group 2: Others simply accepted the death and _____p2_____

Group 3: For others the demise of a loved one led them to a newfound _____q2_____ and a commitment to significantly improve their personal life.

23.

o2. _____

p2. _____

q2. _____

24.

r2. _____

s2. _____

Lessons of Grief

- Compared with other subjects, men who discovered this new meaning in life showed significant improvement in ____r2____ .
- This group also showed a significant advantage in long-term ____s2____

25.

Positive Lessons of Grief Boost Immune System

- This research demonstrated that this newfound sense of purpose can boost the body's immune system as it bolsters the spirit.

Journal of Consulting and Clinical Psychology December 1999

26.

t2. _____

u2. _____

v2. _____

w2. _____

Healthy Grieving

- Not something we experience naturally.
- Worden conceptualizes the grief process as ____t2____
- Tasks imply that there is ____u2____
- This can be ____v2____ to the mourner who feels so ____w2____

Healthy Grieving

Time does not always heal "wounds," but working through them ___x2___ can.

27.

x2. _____

Tasks of Mourning

Task I: Accept the Reality of the Loss

- Communicate about ___y2___
- Have a ___z2___

28.

y2. _____

z2. _____

Tasks of Mourning

Task II: Work Through the Pain

- ___a3___
- Be honest about how you feel.
- Write about the loss.
- Range, L.M. (2002). *Does writing about the bereavement lessen grief…?*

29.

a3. _____

30.

b3. _____

c3. _____

d3. _____

Tasks of Mourning

Task II: Work Through the Pain

- Self-care is important:
  - _____b3_____
  - _____c3_____
  - _____d3_____

31.

e3. _____

f3. _____

Tasks of Mourning

Maintaining Social Ties

Studies have shown _____e3_____ to be more closely
related to later depression than is a history of _____f3_____

32.

Tasks of Mourning

Maintaining Spiritual Ties

Tasks of Mourning

Task II: Use this opportunity to develop more ___g3___

- "Capacity to ____h3____ , difficulty, or inconvenience without complaint. (Roget's)
- "The power of suffering with fortitude; uncomplaining endurance of evils or wrongs, as toil, pain, poverty, insult, oppression, calamity, etc." (American Heritage Dictionary)
- "Run with patience the race that is set before us."

33.

g3. _____

h3. _____

In the full light of day, and in hearing of the music of other voices, the caged bird will not sing the song that his master seeks to teach him. He learns a snatch of this, a trill of that, but never a separate and entire melody. But the master covers the cage, and places it where the bird will listen to the one song he is to sing. In the dark, he tries and tries again to sing that song until it is learned, and he breaks forth in perfect melody. Then the bird is brought forth, and ever after he can sing that song in the light. Thus God deals with His children. He has a song to teach us, and when we have learned it amid the shadows of affliction we can sing it ever afterward. MH 472

34.

Tasks of Mourning

Task III: Adjust to Environment with the Loss

Don't make ____i3____ decisions

35.

i3. _____

36.

j3. _____

k3. _____

Tasks of Mourning

Task III: Adjust to Environment with the Loss

- _____j3_____ that the lost person or thing played in your life.
- Find how these functions can be met_____k3_____

37.

l3. _____

m3. _____

n3. _____

Tasks of Mourning

Task IV: To Emotionally Relocate the Loss

- This does not mean that the loss is _____l3_____
- Reminiscing helps.
- Build on current or new relationships.
- Develop _____m3_____
- Find _____n3_____ and continue old ones.

38.

o3. _____

p3. _____

q3. _____

Tasks of Mourning

Task V: To Grow from the Loss

- Do not settle for _____o3_____
- Honor the lost person or thing by growing from the pain.
- Reflect on what you have _____p3_____ through the loss.
- Let life become more _____q3_____

39.

Tasks of Mourning

Task V: To Grow from the Loss

"And we know that in all things God works for the __r3__ of those who __s3__ him."

Romans 8:28, NIV

r3. _____

s3. _____

40.

Tasks of Mourning

Task V: To Grow from the Loss

How have you grown from loss?

What are some ways you can grow from loss?

41.

Grief Vs. Depression

Grief Complicated by Major Depression:

- Feelings of ____t3____
- Suicidal ideation.
- ____u3____ functioning.
- Prolonged ____v3____

t3. _____

u3. _____

v3. _____

42.

Sometimes life seems hard to bear,
Full of sorrow, trouble, and woe
It's then I have to remember
That it's in the valleys I grow.

If I always stayed on the mountain top
And never experienced pain,
I would never appreciate God's love
And would be living in vain.

43.

I have so much to learn
And my growth is very slow,
Sometimes I need the mountain tops,
But it's in the valley I grow.

I do not always understand
Why things happen as they do,
But I'm very sure of one thing.
My Lord will see me through.

44.

My little valleys are nothing
When I picture Christ on the cross
He went through the valley of death;
His victory was Satan's loss.

Forgive me Lord, for complaining
When I'm feeling so very low.
Just give me a gentle reminder
That's it's in the valleys I grow.

45.

Continue to strengthen me, Lord
And use my life each day
To share your love with others
And help them find their way.

Thank you for valleys, Lord
For this one thing I know
The mountain tops are glorious
But it's in the valley I grow!
—*Jane Eggleston*

46.

Take Comfort

- Loss was ____w3____
- There is a Creator who has made a plan that we should never experience loss, sadness, or death again.
- He is not only ___x3___ He is ____y3____

w3. _____

x3. _____

y3. _____

47.

"Run with patience the race that is set before us."

—Hebrews 12:1

What You Learned

- There are many different types of losses.
- Healthy mourning moves through the stages and tasks of grief or mourning without becoming depression.
- Grief and depression are not the same thing.
- You should not allow cognitive delusions to creep in and influence the way you view the reality of your loss
- In all things, God works for the good of those who love Him.

❧

Daily Dose

Reading Prescription
- *Depression: the Way Out*: Chapter 6: Herbs and Medications, pages 99–119.
- *Telling Yourself the Truth* chapters 13 and 14.
- Chapter of Proverbs (from the Bible) that corresponds with today's date. (Example: July 31, read Proverbs 31.) Also try to read a chapter of Proverbs for each day this week. Circle the verse number or underline in your Bible your favorite proverb in each chapter that you read.

❧

Read "Five Ways to Improve Family Wellness" from page xiii.

Lifestyle Matters

As social beings, we have a serious need for interaction and support from the various important people in our lives. Also important are our jobs, homes, physical property, and vital faculties (like eyesight, hearing, limbs, *etc.*). A loss can be an unexpected blow to the balance of our lives that causes significant upset. An example of this could even be the "death of a vision," such as a couple planning to raise a family, but then being unable to conceive. Learning to deal appropriately with these losses will help us maintain our equilibrium and prevent depression.

- Reflect on a loss you have experienced and its impact on your life. (Some examples of loss are listed in slide 6 from this session's presentation.) *Dr. Nedley spoke in this session about journaling. The space below provides an opportunity to journal your own experience.*

_____

_____

_____

_____

_____

- What beliefs or feelings can you identify in your description above?

- Are any of the beliefs you have about this event or loss cognitive distortions that you can recognize? Write them out using the list of the ten cognitive distortions discussed in the Lifestyle Matters section of Session Four (page 99.)

- Try to understand your experiences in more clear, accurate, truthful, and positive ways.

  (***For example***, if you have lost a loved one you may describe the impact like this: "She was the only one who really loved or understood me; I'll never be able to continue without her. I would probably be better off dead myself." You could more clearly, accurately, truthfully, and positively state the impact in this way: "She was my greatest love and friend and I will miss her dearly. I will draw from the strength and love of my other close relationships to help me get through these hard times. She would certainly want the best for my life and so I will continue to press on and make my life a blessing, for she surely would have wanted that for me.")

- Turn your focus on the blessings that you currently enjoy or have in your life. Write at least three important things you are thankful for in your life:

  _____

  _____

  _____

  _____

- *Analyze What You've Written:* Express your gratitude to God and to those others involved in bringing blessings like these into your life. Make a point to share your appreciation to these individuals this week in person (and by prayer), by phone, or in a letter or e-mail. This will help you to improve your social wellness.

- Individuals without close healthy family members, friends, or church acquaintances nearby with whom they interact several times per week are at higher risk for depression. Overcoming depression and dealing with significant losses in our life requires quality social support. Think of people and activities you feel contribute to your meaningful social support. Incorporate this with the information on page xiv, which discusses ways to improve social wellness.

- It is especially helpful to commit yourself to honorable causes that help others. Some suggestions include involving yourself with community or church projects, church attendance, and other activities consistent with good goals. Do you have any plans for community involvement? If so, share them with the group.

Healthy Lifestyle Scorecard   Week___

Day	Sun	Mon	Tues	Wed	Thur	Fri	Sat
Date							
Exercise *Beginning and ending times for exercise sessions.*							
Sleep *Beginning and ending times for sleep.*							
Deep Breathing *Beginning and ending times for when you practiced deep breathing.*							
Avoided Negative Speech *Beginning and ending times for when you avoided negative speech.*							
Water *How many ounces of water you drank in a day, along with the times of day.*							
Spiritual Activity *Daily time reading Proverbs and praying. Also, write what time(s).*							
Favorite Verse							
Classical Music *Beginning and ending times for when you listened to classical music.*							
Sunlight *Beginning and ending times for sunlight or lightbox use.*							

Session Eight
How to Improve Brain Function

DURING this session, pay attention to:

- How your brain is affected by everything you process.
- The positive mental benefits that a plant-based diet imparts.
- Whether you make use of the greatest aid—the Bible.
- What you can do to protect and enhance your frontal lobe.

Your *Workbook* contains the slides from Dr. Nedley's PowerPoint™ presentation for **Session Eight.** Please follow along as you watch the DVD.

DVD PowerPoint™ Slides
Session Eight
How to Improve Brain Function

WHILE watching Dr. Nedley's presentation, follow along with these slides that match those used in the session. If you want to, you can fill in the blanks for the missing words—sometimes a blank equals one word, other times it equals a short phrase. Use the blanks in the margins with letters that correspond to the letters on the blanks on the PowerPoint™ slides to match your answers. (For example, for blank [a] write the answer on the line to the side of the slide marked [a.], and so on.) Answers can be found in the back of this workbook.

1.

DEPRESSION RECOVERY

How to Improve Brain Function

2.

The Ten "Hit" Categories

1. Genetic
2. Developmental
3. Lifestyle
4. Circadian rhythm
5. Addiction
6. Nutrition
7. Toxic
8. Social/Complicated Grief
9. Medical Condition
10. Frontal Lobe

9. Common Medical Hits

- Hepatitis C
- Recent head injury
- Stroke
- Terminal Cancer
- Parkinson's
- Uncontrolled ____a____
- ____b____

- Congestive Heart Failure
- Postpartum severe stress
- Premenstrual Tension Syndrome
- Inadequately treated thyroid disease
- Inadequately treated adrenal gland disease

3.

a. _____

b. _____

Research in the 1990s and 2000s

It is now well established that one of the main characteristics of virtually all depressed individuals—no matter what the underlying cause—is a significant decrease in the frontal lobe's blood flow and activity.

Pet Scan

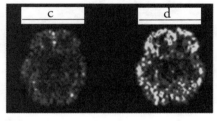

4.

c. _____

d. _____

What Really Comes First?

Drevets presents compelling evidence that frontal lobe problems are the ____e____ and the effects are depressive ____f____.

5.

e. _____

f. _____

g. _____

h. _____

i. _____

6.

The Frontal Lobe

- Scientific studies show the frontal lobe is the seat of
  - _____g_____
  - _____h_____
  - _____i_____

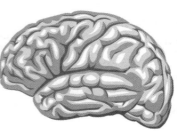

7.

THE LOBES OF THE BRAIN

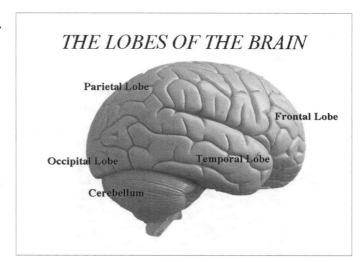

8.

j. _____

k. _____

l. _____

Frontal Lobe Size

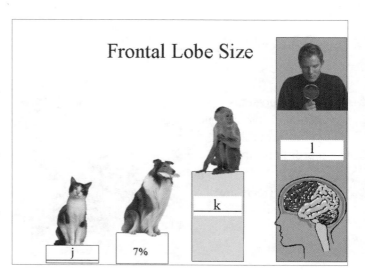

Effects of Compromised Frontal Lobes

- Impairment of ____m____
- Social impairment (loss of love for family)
- Lack of ____n____
- Abstract reasoning impaired
- Mathematical understanding diminished
- Loss of ____o____
- Lack of ____p____

9.

m. _____

n. _____

o. _____

p. _____

What the Frontal Lobe Desires

_____q_____ are used almost exclusively by the brain for optimal function.

10.

q. _____

The Superior Diet

11.

171

12.

r. _____

s. _____

Sugar and the Brain

Large amounts of ___r___ in the diet have been demonstrated to impair ___s___ functions in school age children.

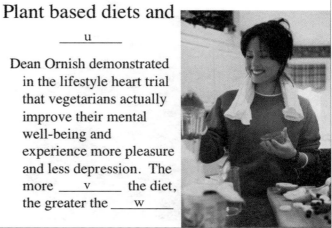

13.

_____t_____ Acid Decreases Ability

t. _____

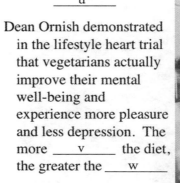

14.

u. _____

v. _____

w. _____

Plant based diets and ___u___

Dean Ornish demonstrated in the lifestyle heart trial that vegetarians actually improve their mental well-being and experience more pleasure and less depression. The more ___v___ the diet, the greater the ___w___

Hypnosis

Hypnosis attempts to cancel out frontal lobe functions and bring people into ___x___ in which they are highly suggestible.

This is most easily accomplished by training the eyes to focus in on ___y___, the best object being a little flickering light.

The person will record information and duties without interpretation, or without frontal lobe activity.

15.

x. _____

y. _____

Music

Music enters the brain through its ___z___ regions, which include the ___a2___ lobe and limbic system.

16.

z. _____

a2. _____

From there, some kinds of ___b2___ tend to produce a frontal lobe response that influences the will, ___c2___ , and reasoning power.

17.

b2. _____

c2. _____

18.

d2. _____

e2. _____

f2. _____

___d2___ music is not necessarily ___e2___ music.

Other kinds of music will evoke very little, if any, frontal lobe response, but will produce a large emotional response with very little logical or ___f2___ interpretation.

19.

g2. _____

h2. _____

Constant Stimulation of the Senses

"Constant stimulation of the senses shuts down the ___g2___ processes, and ultimately shuts down the ability to face life ___h2___ This leads to escape techniques that involve withdrawal, apathy, and rejection of disciplined thinking when faced with difficult duties and decisions."

Alvin Toffler

20.

i2. _____

j2. _____

k2. _____

l2. _____

Definite Frontal Lobe Hits

- Alcohol, nicotine, ___i2___
- ___j2___ diet
- Frequent ___k2___ outside of marriage
- MTV viewer
- Undergoing ___l2___
- No regular Scriptural study or abstract thinking
- Habitually going against your conscience

21.

General Treatment Measures For Depression

That Improve Frontal Lobe Function

22.

___m2___ Therapy Lifts ___n2___

Music psychotherapy, in which people are encouraged to reflect on their past, present and future while listening to classical music, improves mood and reduces stress.

Six sessions of classical music therapy were held over a 12 week period in 23 to 45 year-olds. These subjects showed:

- Improved scores on test of overall mood
- Reported feeling less depressed
- Reported feeling less fatigue
- ___o2___ improved (dropped)

McCabe, PM. Health Psychology. 1997;16:390-400.

m2. _____

n2. _____

o2. _____

23.

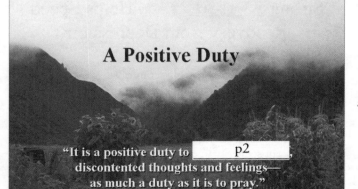

A Positive Duty

"It is a positive duty to ___p2___, discontented thoughts and feelings— as much a duty as it is to pray."

MH 251

p2. _____

24.

A Positive Duty

25.

q2. _____

r2. _____

s2. _____

Take Care of Your Frontal Lobe

- Protect it from mechanical injury
- Supply it with good ____q2____
- Give it good nutrition
- Get adequate ____r2____
- Exercise it
- Control the ____s2____
- Prevent or control disease that affects it

26.

t2. _____

u2. _____

v2. _____

Strong _____t2_____ Helps Speed Recovery from Depression

"Depressed patients with higher intrinsic ____u2____ scores had more rapid remissions than patients with lower scores."

Patients recovered from depression 70 percent sooner with every 10 point increase in the religiosity assessment score. ____v2____ religious activity had much less of an impact.

American Journal of Psychiatry. 1998;155:536-542.

Acts 17

11 These were more noble than those in
Thessalonica, in that they received the word
with all _____w2_____ , and searched the
scriptures daily, whether those things were
so.

27.

w2. _____

Providing Great Inputs

"The Bible, _____x2_____ , is to be our
guide."

28.

x2. _____

"Nothing is so calculated to enlarge
the mind and strengthen the intellect
as the _y2_ of the Bible."

29.

y2. _____

30.

The Bible

"No other study will so elevate the soul and give vigor to the faculties as the study of the living oracles…"

31.

z2. _____

a3. _____

b3. _____

"As the __z2__ is brought to the study of God's Word…

…the understanding will ___a3___
…the higher power will develop for the ____b3____ of high and ennobling truth."

MCP 93

32.

c3. _____

d3. _____

e3. _____

Do You Want To?

- Be more intelligent
- Be more analytical
- Make better ___c3___
- Have a greater capacity to empathize with others
- Have better discernment
- Improve your ___d3___

- Have greater ability to see into the future
- Have greater ability to overcome an addiction
- Have greater power to follow your conscience
- Be more open to understanding and doing the ___e3___

33.

Romans 12

1 I beseech you therefore, brethren, by the mercies of God, that ye present your bodies a living sacrifice, holy, acceptable unto God, which is your reasonable service.

2 And be not conformed to this world: but be ye transformed by the renewing of your mind, that ye may prove what is that good, and acceptable, and perfect, will of God.

34.

Treatment for Depression

Ps 34:19

19 Many are the ____f3____ of the ____g3____ but the LORD ____h3____ him out of them all.

Hebrews 12:11-13

11 Now no chastening for the present seemeth to be joyous, but grievous: nevertheless afterward it yieldeth the peaceable fruit of righteousness unto them which are exercised thereby.

12 Wherefore lift up the hands which hang down, and the feeble knees;

13 And make straight paths for your feet, lest that which is lame be turned out of the way; but let it rather be healed.

f3. _____

g3. _____

h3. _____

35.

____i3____ for Depression

- Attempt to find the cause
- Enhance frontal lobe ____j3____
- ____k3____ frontal lobe suppressants
- Increase brain serotonin levels
- Sufficient ____l3____ intake
- Sufficient folate intake
- Sufficient B vitamin intake

i3. _____

j3. _____

k3. _____

l3. _____

36.

m3. _____

n3. _____

o3. _____

Treatments for Depression

- _____m3_____ exercises
- Classical __n3__ therapy
- Avoid ____o3____ thinking
- Increase faith and devotion to God

37.

p3. _____

q3. _____

r3. _____

Recommend a Study of the Book of Daniel

- Each chapter begins with a
  _____p3_____ and transitions into an
  _____q3_____ !
- Applying the principles of each chapter
  reveals keys for _____r3_____ .
- The last six chapters deals with
  symbols, prophecy, and high abstract
  thought.
- Sure to improve frontal lobe function!

38.

s3. _____

t3. _____

u3. _____

Follow-up Plans

You have a ____s3____, but ____t3____,
it's a __u3__ cure!

39.

In Closing

- "We love you, Depression Recovery Seminar Participants!"
- We hope this will prove helpful to each of you. Every person here is ___v3___

v3. _____

- May "the LORD bless you and ___w3___

w3. _____

- the LORD make His face to shine upon you, and be gracious to you;
- the LORD lift up His ___x3___ upon you, and give you peace." Numbers 6:24-26

x3. _____

৶

What You Learned

- Decreased blood flow to the frontal lobe exists in virtually all depressed patients.
- A plant-based diet is the best for mental health.
- Attentive listening to classical music has an enormous, positive impact on the frontal lobe.
- Scripture and religious faith aid in mental health and intellect— along with developing a deeper understanding of man's place in the world in relation to God—which should be of great aid to those experiencing depression.

Daily Dose

Reading Prescription
- *Depression: the Way Out:* Chapter 9, The Frontal Lobe of the Brain, and review Chapter 10.
- Chapter of Proverbs (from the Bible) that corresponds with today's date. (Example: July 31, read Proverbs 31.) Also try to read a chapter of Proverbs for each day this week. Circle the verse number or underline in your Bible your favorite proverb in each chapter that you read.

Lifestyle Matters

1. **Review all the activities you have been asked to do throughout the seven previous weekly sessions.** Are you applying these concepts in your life? Evaluate yourself with the chart below using the following scale, circling the appropriate letter (A, B, or C). *(The superscript number following each item indicates the session where each Lifestyle Matter is found.)*

A I have *habitually changed/added/been consistent* with these activities.

B I have *half-heartedly changed or added* these activities to my schedule.

C I have *yet to change or add* these activities to my weekly routine.

Scale

No critical or negative speech[1]	A B C
Classical music therapy[1]	A B C
Exercise and intermittent training (I.T.)[1,2]	A B C
Adequate water intake[1]	A B C
Deep breathing exercises[2]	A B C
Light therapy; good light exposure[2]	A B C
Massage[2]	A B C
Contrast showers[2]	A B C
Tryptophan intake[3]	A B C
Vitamin B_{12} intake[3]	A B C
Omega-3 intake[3]	A B C
Folic acid intake[3]	A B C
Cholesterol intake reduced/eliminated[3]	A B C
Plant-based diet[3]	A B C
Thought reconstruction exercises[4]	A B C
Kicking habits[5]	A B C
Calcium intake[6]	A B C
Melatonin intake[6]	A B C
Proper sleep habits[6]	A B C
Stages and tasks of grief and loss[7]	A B C
Social involvement[7]	A B C

2. **For all the activities above for which you circled (A), great job!** Keep up with this program and you will continue to improve until your depression is at last completely under control. What is your plan to continue with your wonderful progress? Choose someone who can help you stay with it if your determination should begin to wane.

_____

_____

_____

_____

3. **What is your plan to improve on all the items that you circled (B)?** By following the recommendations on the scorecard, you will continue to improve your healthy lifestyle.

_____

_____

_____

_____

4. Review page 182 for each item circled (C) that you have not yet begun to implement. What is your plan for changing your lifestyle? Remember the tools that we have talked about throughout the *Depression Recovery Program*. Think about how you can use each one of these tools to contribute towards success. *Review the sections pertaining to these activities in order to make sure you understand the reasons these exercises are crucial to depression recovery.*

_____

_____

_____

_____

_____

_____

_____

5. **Fill out your "After" Depression Self Test.** Make sure to put your full name, address, and phone number.

6. **Now please complete your final Depression, Anxiety, and EQ Assessment, carefully answering each question.** Make sure to put your full name, address, and date of birth on the front of the sheet. We appreciate your cooperation in this, as it will provide vital information we will use for improving treatment for all those who have depression. Thank you for your assistance in making our program (and subsequent *Depression Recovery* products) the best that they can be.

If you are attending a community program, the program director will have these collected so that they can be evaluated.

Important Dates to Remember

In the space below, write the dates for the follow-up *Depression Recovery* Alumni meetings and additional programs you may be interested in attending.

_____

_____

_____

_____

_____

_____

_____

_____

_____

_____

Depression Self Test—"After"

Reflect over the previous two weeks and rate the following symptoms:
(Circle the appropriate number for each item.)

	A None	B Questionable	C Mild	D Definite
1. Deep sadness or feelings of emptiness; feeling down or hopeless.	0	1	2	3
2. Decreased interest or pleasure in nearly all activities.	0	1	2	3
3. Decrease or increase in appetite; or unusual loss or gain in weight.	0	1	2	3
4. Sleep habits have changed; sleeping more or less than usual.	0	1	2	3
5. Others (or you) have noticed your physical movements or speech have been slower than normal; or instead that you have more agitation or irritation with yourself or others.	0	1	2	3
6. Experiencing fatigue or loss of energy; feeling tired often.	0	1	2	3
7. Experiencing feelings of worthlessness, inappropriate guilt, or that you are a failure.	0	1	2	3
8. Decrease in ability to think or concentrate on common tasks or difficulty making good decisions.	0	1	2	3
9. Thinking about death often or considering harming yourself or others.	0	1	2	3

Self-Scoring the Depression Self Test

Add the numbers from each column above, and place the totals in the corresponding boxes here—then add across to determine your final symptom score for the Self Test.

Examples: Since column A is always equal to 0 (zero), this blank is already filled with a zero. If you circle four "1"s in column B, then your total for that column is "4". If you circle three "2"s in column C, then your total for that column is "6". If you circle nine "3"s in column D, then your total for that column is "27". *(These are all hypothetical totals.)*

A __0__ + B _____ + C _____ + D _____ = _____
                                                    Total Score

If you answered B, C, or D for Question 9, be sure to see a health professional *as soon as possible,* even if it means going to the local Emergency Room.

Major depression is a concern if you have answered questions 1 or 2 with B, C, or D *and* have a score as indicated below:

0–6 .... None
7–10 .... Mild
11–19 .... Moderate
20 or above .... Severe

Please Note: Having recently faced a dramatic emotional crisis or loss can cause situational depression or bereavement. **This test is not designed to replace the competent evaluation of a health professional.**

Have you taken Dr. Nedley's Comprehensive Depression, Anxiety, and EQ Assessment? It's the last step in finishing this course. Ask your director or refer to page 19.

Healthy Lifestyle Scorecard   Week ___

Day	Sun	Mon	Tues	Wed	Thur	Fri	Sat
Date							
Exercise *Beginning and ending times for exercise sessions.*							
Sleep *Beginning and ending times for sleep.*							
Deep Breathing *Beginning and ending times for when you practiced deep breathing.*							
Avoided Negative Speech *Beginning and ending times for when you avoided negative speech.*							
Water *How many ounces of water you drank in a day, along with the times of day.*							
Spiritual Activity *Daily time reading Proverbs and praying. Also, write what time(s).*							
Favorite Verse							
Classical Music *Beginning and ending times for when you listened to classical music.*							
Sunlight *Beginning and ending times for sunlight or lightbox use.*							

Additional Resources

Healthy Lifestyle Scorecard   Week ___

Day	Sun	Mon	Tues	Wed	Thur	Fri	Sat
Date							
Exercise *Beginning and ending times for exercise sessions.*							
Sleep *Beginning and ending times for sleep.*							
Deep Breathing *Beginning and ending times for when you practiced deep breathing.*							
Avoided Negative Speech *Beginning and ending times for when you avoided negative speech.*							
Water *How many ounces of water you drank in a day, along with the times of day.*							
Spiritual Activity *Daily time reading Proverbs and praying. Also, write what time(s).*							
Favorite Verse							
Classical Music *Beginning and ending times for when you listened to classical music.*							
Sunlight *Beginning and ending times for sunlight or lightbox use.*							

Healthy Lifestyle Scorecard   Week ___

Day	Sun	Mon	Tues	Wed	Thur	Fri	Sat
Date							
Exercise *Beginning and ending times for exercise sessions.*							
Sleep *Beginning and ending times for sleep.*							
Deep Breathing *Beginning and ending times for when you practiced deep breathing.*							
Avoided Negative Speech *Beginning and ending times for when you avoided negative speech.*							
Water *How many ounces of water you drank in a day, along with the times of day*							
Spiritual Activity *Daily time reading Proverbs and praying. Also, write what time(s).*							
Favorite Verse							
Classical Music *Beginning and ending times for when you listened to classical music.*							
Sunlight *Beginning and ending times for sunlight or lightbox use.*							

Healthy Lifestyle Scorecard   Week ___

Day	Sun	Mon	Tues	Wed	Thur	Fri	Sat
Date							
Exercise *Beginning and ending times for exercise sessions.*							
Sleep *Beginning and ending times for sleep.*							
Deep Breathing *Beginning and ending times for when you practiced deep breathing.*							
Avoided Negative Speech *Beginning and ending times for when you avoided negative speech.*							
Water *How many ounces of water you drank in a day, along with the times of day.*							
Spiritual Activity *Daily time reading Proverbs and praying. Also, write what time(s).*							
Favorite Verse							
Classical Music *Beginning and ending times for when you listened to classical music.*							
Sunlight *Beginning and ending times for sunlight or lightbox use.*							

Answer Keys for Depression Recovery Program PowerPoint® Fill in the Blank Questions

Session One: Identifying Depression and Its Causes
a) 1915
b) 25
c) 20 million
d) billion
e) one
f) four
g) one
h) eight
i) situational
j) depression
k) serious loss
l) never diagnosed with the condition
m) cure
n) identified
o) cause
p) found
q) very possible
r) apathy
s) lack of concentration
t) morbid thoughts
u) sadness
v) emptiness
w) weeks
x) depressed
y) increase
z) decrease
a2) appetite
b2) sleep more
c2) sleep less
d2) falling asleep
e2) early awakening
f2) agitated or irritated
g2) physical movements
h2) slower
i2) fatigue
j2) loss of energy
k2) worthlessness
l2) excessive
m2) inappropriate guilt
n2) concentrate
o2) decisions
p2) thoughts of death
q2) someone else
r2) seriously
s2) attempted
t2) significant loss
u2) subsyndromal depression
v2) stroke
w2) heart disease
x2) risk of suicide
y2) headache

z2) osteoporosis
a3) addictive behavior
b3) anger or hostility
c3) asthma
d3) offspring
e3) sex hormones
f3) memory
g3) diagnosis
h3) cause
i3) identify the causes
j3) systematically
k3) prescribing a drug
l3) all-fronts attack
m3) 5 separate genes
n3) first degree
o3) DNA testing
p3) both biological parents
q3) sexual abuse
r3) nutritional
s3) puberty
t3) twice
u3) panic or eating disorders
v3) lower protein
w3) higher protein
x3) animal protein
y3) menstrual period
z3) vegetable
a4) much later onset
b4) modifiable
c4) addictions
d4) from medication
e4) those who adhere
f4) the brain
g4) choices
h4) relationships
i4) joy
j4) clean fun
k4) true success

Session Two: Lifestyle Treatment for Depression
a) exercise program
b) 30 minutes a day
c) breathing fresh air
d) physical activity
e) long brisk walks
f) 7 days minimum
g) interval training
h) unfit
i) athlete
j) heart
k) rest

l) resume
m) serotonin
n) awakening
o) partum and post-partum
p) muscle
q) metabolic
r) atrophy
s) intolerance
t) blood oxygen
u) additive
v) regular insomnia
w) sleeping
x) eating
y) clear
z) improves
a2) returns
b2) zombi
c2) awaken with the sun
d2) 10 minutes
e2) no noise
f2) be still
g2) eyes closed
h2) anxiety
i2) perceived stress
j2) nothing
k2) avoid negative thinking
l2) something critical
m2) over again
n2) health of body
o2) gratitude
p2) praise
q2) lifestyle

Session Three: Nutrition and the Brain
a) overlooked cause
b) nutrition change
c) 3 to 6 months
d) carbohydrate
e) obvious clues
f) tryptophan
g) tryptophan
h) omega-3 fatty acid
i) omega-3
j) manic
k) omega-3
l) walnuts, ground
m) or brown sugar
n) omega-3 fatty acid
o) low folate levels
p) folate
q) custard mixes
r) pancake mixes

s) parmesan cheese
t) lard
u) vitamin B6
v) sweet bell peppers
w) marked anorexia
x) energy levels
y) 5 pounds
z) improved energy
a2) intake
b2) expenditure
c2) 3500 calories
d2) good breakfast
e2) evening meal
f2) 45 minutes
g2) less than
h2) nutrients
i2) lead levels
j2) drinking water
k2) calcium supplements
l2) mercury levels
m2) bismuth
n2) equivalency
o2) antidepressants
p2) improving your diet
q2) food addictions

Session Four: How Thinking Can Defeat Depression

a) a pill
b) lasting relief
c) most common
d) cured
e) do not improve
f) medication
g) 2 years
h) continue medication
i) ultimate solution
j) severe depression
k) discontinuation
l) crying
m) hostility
n) social affiliations
o) impulsiveness
p) decreasing alarm
q) counseling
r) psychotherapy
s) superior
t) placebo
u) chronic
v) twenty
w) 85
x) personal responsibility
y) past events
z) do differently
a2) Aaron Beck
b2) Albert Ellis
c2) drug therapy

d2) more likely
e2) brain chemistry
f2) depression
g2) anorexia
h2) thought or perception
i2) very moment
j2) how you feel
k2) depressed
l2) discouraged
m2) angry
n2) annoyed
o2) optimistic
p2) interested
q2) messages
r2) how you feel
s2) happening
t2) unfulfilled
u2) gross distortions
v2) suffering
w2) activating
x2) belief
y2) consequence
z2) all-or-nothing
a3) mental filter
b3) mind reading
c3) fortune-teller
d3) emotional
e3) personalization
f3) worthless
g3) not worthless
h3) bonus
i3) worthwhile
j3) misbelief breakers
k3) painful thoughts
l3) other ways
m3) scriptural material
n3) truth
o3) simple, not easy
p3) misbeliefs
q3) practice the truth
r3) God does
s3) manage my life
t3) evidence
u3) what would I say
v3) reconstruct your thinking
w3) renewing of your mind
x3) true
y3) positive thinking
z3) believe
a4) acknowledge
b4) hard to find
c4) depressed
d4) a long time
e4) before
f4) write a letter to yourself
g4) memorize scripture
h4) feeling better
i4) getting better

j4) practice, practice, practice
k4) heart

Session Five: Positive Lifestyle Choices

a) what to do
b) ready to do it
c) doing it
d) contemplation
e) preparation
f) action
g) maintenance
h) marijuana user
i) smoker or tobacco user
j) heavy caffeine user
k) illicit drug user
l) addictions
m) alcohol
n) narcotics
o) moderation
p) healthy
q) abstinence
r) unhealthy
s) unhealthy
t) addictive
u) unhealthy substances
v) continually use
w) increased amounts
x) dependence
y) relapse
z) compulsive
a2) alcoholic
b2) nicotine addict
c2) abstinence for life
d2) bad habit
e2) enjoyment
f2) kept alive
g2) permanently abandoned
h2) will not be missed
i2) misery
j2) choose not to smoke
k2) caffeine
l2) high risk
m2) destructive
n2) spiritual resources
o2) let God
p2) victory
q2) Jesus Christ
r2) ask
s2) gift
t2) more
u2) ask
v2) faith
w2) fail
x2) with the same mind
y2) in the flesh
z2) the will of God

a3) victory
b3) warning
c3) Redeemer
d3) habits
e3) culture
f3) choices and values

Session Six: Stress without Distress
a) pineal
b) pineal gland
c) serotonin
d) melatonin
e) fall
f) melatonin
g) radiation
h) tumors
i) immune
j) stress
k) pleasure
l) osteoporosis
m) two hours
n) four hours
o) tryptophan
p) serotonin
q) melatonin
r) banana
s) ginger
t) stress
u) caffeine
v) alcohol
w) tobacco
x) stress
y) good
z) secretory proteins
a2) cancer cells
b2) immune response
c2) big bad thing
d2) unusually prolonged
e2) reducing
f2) seeking
g2) active stress
h2) responded to
i2) immune system
j2) sleep aids
k2) vitamin B12
l2) antidepressants
m2) natural light
n2) artificial light
o2) vitamin B6
p2) alarm reaction
q2) state of resistance
r2) stage of exhaustion
s2) stress
t2) major
u2) illnesses
v2) asthma

w2) reproductive
x2) eczema
y2) avoid or remove
z2) ignoring
a3) lifestyle
b3) herbs
c3) stress
d3) lavender
e3) appetite
f3) lemon balm
g3) valerian
h3) medications
i3) Prozac®
j3) Buspar®
k3) continually
l3) bones
m3) honorable cause
n3) planning
o3) for the morrow
p3) good
q3) earnest prayer
r3) nothing
s3) not distressed
t3) not in despair
u3) but not forsaken
v3) more than conquerors
w3) heavy laden
x3) rest
y3) trivial
z3) trust God

Session Seven: Living Above Loss
a) social support
b) alcoholic or drug addict
c) grief
d) mourning
e) a body part
f) a job
g) loved one
h) legitimate
i) negative feelings
j) reality
k) distortions
l) enhance
m) defeat
n) grieving process
o) healing
p) grief
q) depression
r) of numbness
s) denial of the loss
t) screaming
u) 3 to 12
v) sleeping
w) digestive problems
x) fatigue
y) anger
z) guilt

a2) depressive
b2) clearer
c2) consequences
d2) month by month
e2) new habits
f2) lifestyle
g2) wise plans for the future
h2) good news
i2) charge
j2) activity
k2) introspection
l2) reaffirmation
m2) cognitive processing
n2) different conclusions
o2) negative aspects of life
p2) moved on
q2) respect for life
r2) immune function
s2) survival
t2) tasks
u2) work to do
v2) empowering
w2) helpless
x2) over time
y2) the loss
z2) mourning ritual
a3) do not avoid the pain
b3) adequate sleep
c3) balanced diet
d3) exercise
e3) poor social support
f3) torture
g3) patience
h3) endure hardship
i3) life-changing
j3) identify the roles
k3) now
l3) forgotten
m3) new routines
n3) new interests
o3) surviving
p3) learned or gained
q3) meaningful
r3) good
s3) love
t3) worthlessness
u3) grossly impaired
v3) bereavement
w3) never meant to be
x3) Creator
y3) Re-Creator

Session Eight: How to Improve Brain Function
a) diabetes
b) lupus
c) depressed

d) recovered
e) cause
f) symptoms
g) spirituality
h) morality
i) the will
j) 3.5%
k) 17%
l) 33%
m) moral principle
n) foresight
o) empathy
p) restraint
q) carbohydrates
r) sugar
s) frontal lobe
t) arachidonic
u) mood
v) plant based
w) benefit
x) a trance
y) one object
z) emotional
a2) temporal
b2) music

c2) moral worth
d2) upbeat
e2) uplifting
f2) moral
g2) analytical
h2) rationally
i2) illicit drugs
j2) low carbohydrate
k2) sexual arousal
l2) hypnosis
m2) music
n2) mood
o2) cortisol levels
p2) resist melancholy
q2) oxygen
r2) sunshine
s2) inputs
t2) religious faith
u2) religiosity
v2) external
w2) readiness of mind
x2) just as it reads
y2) study
z2) mind
a3) enlarge

b3) comprehension
c3) decisions
d3) mood
e3) will of God
f3) afflictions
g3) righteous
h3) delivereth
i3) treatments
j3) function
k3) avoid
l3) omega-3
m3) breathing
n3) music
o3) negative
p3) disappointment
q3) appointment
r3) long lasting success
s3) great start
t3) remember
u3) 20 week
v3) important
w3) keep you
x3) countenance

Thank You

Thank you for purchasing the *Nedley Depression Recovery Program.* Your participation in this comprehensive program can benefit others as well as yourself. Please take the time to fill out this final questionnaire so that we may better understand the many facets of this challenging disease. Your information is strictly confidential and will help us more successfully and quickly help others to a healthier, happier life.

Remember, it can take up to 20 weeks for the positive changes that you have made to bring maximum positive results. Continue with your new life in positive thinking, healthful eating, exercising, sunlight, rest, fresh air, water, and reflection with a spiritual focus (such as the reading of Holy Scripture) to maximize your potential for a lasting cure.

—Neil Nedley, M.D.

Lyrics to Depression Recovery Songs

I Don't Like It

I don't like it.
I don't like it.
It's OK. It's OK.
I can stand it anyway,
I can stand it anyway.
I'm all right.
I'm all right.

Feelings (To the Tune of Yankee Doodle)

Feelings come and
Feelings go and
Feelings are deceiving,
Trust alone on the word of God,
It's something worth believing.

'Cause feelings come and
Feelings go and
Feelings are deceiving,
Trust alone on the word of God,
It's something worth believing.

I Surrender All†

All to Jesus I surrender,
every thought I bring to You,
casting down imaginations,
captive only to what's true.

I surrender all!
I surrender all!
You desire Truth within me;
I surrender all.

All to Jesus I surrender.
What I think will certainly
shape perceptions of experience,
and become a part of me.

I surrender all!
I surrender all!
You desire Truth within me;
I surrender all.
True and honest, just and pure,
and lovely things of good report,
if there's virtue, if there's praise,
my thoughts will only be these sort.

I surrender all!
I surrender all!
You desire Truth within me;
I surrender all.

I'm drawn by my fallen feelings to regret, so
I must test.
Use my will, and reason, conscience;
am I worshipping the Best?

I surrender all!
I surrender all!

What I live for is my Master,
I surrender all.

When I fear that I'm worth nothing,
there's a Truth that sets me free:
I am valued by the price paid,
GOD HIMSELF has died for me!

I surrender all;
intimate to You,
"knowing" Truth
is more than knowledge,
I surrender all.

† Lyrics to "I Surrender All" and "Onward Christian Soldiers" © 2005 by Anthea Hii. Anthea requests that these lyrics only be used in connection with the Nedley Depression Recovery Program in order to help others in their recovery from Depression. Used by permission.

Onward Christian Soldiers†

Onward, Christian soldiers!
Marching as to war,
Fighting false perceptions,
Feelings, pride, and more.
Christ has given battle tools:
Reason, conscience, TRUTH!
Forward into battle,
Use our WILLS to choose!

Onward, Christian soldiers!
Marching as to war,

With the cross of Jesus
Going on before.

When the Spirit of truth is come,
To all truth He guides.
There is comfort, peace with truth;
There is none with lies.
By deception, Satan gains
Power o'er the mind.
Through the Word of Truth, the Spirit
Subdues humankind.

Onward, Christian soldiers!
Marching as to war,
With the words of Jesus
Going on before.

Minds are much like gardens;
Seeds of truth can sprout.
We must tend them constantly;
Weeds can choke them out.
Gardening is no easy task!
We must do our part.
Christians must be vigilant -
Life's a battle march!

Onward, Christian soldiers -
Women men and youth,
Every thought we must yield
To the Spirit of truth.

† Lyrics to "I Surrender All" and "Onward Christian Soldiers" © 2005 by Anthea Hii. Anthea requests that these lyrics only be used in connection with the Nedley Depression Recovery Program in order to help others in their recovery from Depression. Used by permission.